R. Gupta's®

A Flying Start

Your career in airlines

with

Focus on Cabin Crew

By

Benu Berry
Ex Airline, Experienced Trainer in Aviation

Anjani A Gupta
Author of Career Books

Ramesh Publishing House

NEW DELHI

Published by:
O.P. Gupta
for Ramesh Publishing House
Admin. Office: 12-H, New Daryaganj Road,
Opp. Traffic Kotwali,
New Delhi-110002
✆ 23261567, 23275224
Telefax: 011-23275124
EMail: info@rameshpublishinghouse.com
Website: www.rameshpublishinghouse.com
Showroom:
- 4457, Nai Sarak, Delhi-6
✆ 23918938, 23918532
- 2604/16, Balaji Market,
Nai Sarak, Delhi-6 ✆ 23253720

Ist Edition: April, 2010

ISBN 81-7819-947-1

R-1253

Price: Rs. 110/- only

Printed at:
Chetna Printers
Delhi

Contents

★ ★ ★

A FLYING START

1. Introduction to Aviation Sector

AVIATION industry in India is one of the fastest growing industries in the world. With the liberalisation of the Indian Aviation Sector, it has undergone a rapid transformation. From being primarily a government-owned industry, the Indian aviation industry is now dominated by privately-owned full service airlines and low-cost carriers.

Earlier, air travel was a privilege only a few could afford, but today, it is within the scope of a larger number of citizens.

The aviation industry traces its history to 1912, with the first flight from Karachi to Delhi, done by Indian State Air Services & Imperial Airways (UK), an extension of the London-Karachi flight.

Mr. J.R.D. Tata, India's leading industrialist, had acquired an A-licence in 1932. He himself flew a single engine Puss Moth, carrying postal mail of Imperial Airways, from Karachi to Mumbai via Ahmadabad. An RAF pilot, Neville Vincent then flew it to Madras.

With the outbreak of World War II, airline progress in Asia came to a relative halt, with aircraft being drafted for military aid. Regular commercial service was restored when WWII ended. Tata Airlines became a Pvt. Ltd. Co. in 1946, called Air India. It was a transport company providing both cargo and passenger services. After independence, the airline was acquired by the Government of India. The airline was granted status of operating internationally under AI International.

On 8th June 1948, the first international flight from Mumbai to London flew via Cairo and Geneva. Jet services to New York via London began in 1960. On the 8th June 1948, it became the first all-jet airline.

In 1953, Government of India nationalised all existing assets, forming Indian Air Corporation for domestic routes and Air India International for international services. Until 1991, they had monopoly in India. Private airlines were allowed an air taxi scheme, under which they could operate chartered and non-scheduled services for the upliftment of Indian tourism. This act was repealed in 1994 and private carriers obtained permission to operate scheduled flights.

Indian aviation industry witnessed a major change in 2003 when Air Deccan introduced budget flying by lowering fares to a mere 17% of what the other airlines were charging. Spicejet, Goair, Kingfisher Red, Paramount have now major market shares and have set new trends in India.

Industry statistics have shown a growth curve that establishes the emergence of India as a new world leader, even ahead of China and Europe. Domestic traffic is expected to increase income by 15% annually. Four hundred and eighty aircraft are on order. As tourism increases, more aircraft will be required as well as crew.

An overview of the aviation industry gives the following categories for analysis:

1. **Airlines in India:** Airlines in India are managed by the Ministry of Civil Aviation, Government of India. All operating commercial airlines have to obtain a licence to operate. The Federation of Indian Airlines deals with challenges in domestic segment and establishes new trends.
2. **Airports in India:** In order to establish international standards in operational, terminal and cargo services, the International Airports Authority of India was fused with National Airports Authority to become Airport Authority of India (AAI). It is responsible for all infrastructure- and maintenance-related tasks. All airports come under its purview.
3. **Aviation Schools in India:** Since aviation provides lucrative careers, it's a major attraction. For professional training of these enthusiasts, various academies are providing cabin crew, ground staff, as well as commercial pilot (CPL) training. Ticketing and reservation, hospitality, customer services are also covered.

The future outlook of the Indian aviation industry depends to a great extent on the various institutes operational in the country. The aviation industry research undertaken by the Ministry of Civil Aviation ensures technological advances.

The initial airliners were actually mail planes, with few extra seats for passengers. The only crews were pilots, who were too busy flying the planes. Imperial airways first had teenagers to mainly board luggage and reassure various people on the plane. In 1930, Ellen Church, a registered nurse, along with Boeing, proposed that the cabin crew should be registered nurses to look after any sick passenger. This became an integral part of the airline industry, but it was relaxed during World War II, as so many were recruited in the armed forces. Although it was a perfectly respectable career, it was an underpaid job, subservient to the pilots. Later, cabin crew members and representatives of the equal flight movement brought change with regard to these problems.

There are a few people who dream to have their workspace in the sky; for them, sky is the limit. With a remarkable growth in the aviation industry, a plethora of career opportunities knock the door.

Young enthusiasts who have energy, stamina and calibre to turn their dream into reality, aviation sector is best suited for them. Career options in aviation are very rewarding and challenging to top it, the remuneration and other benefits are really enviable as compared to other job options. The jobs pay handsome hefty amounts but for that you need to know your aptitude. Aviation sector has opened avenues for Pilots, Co-Pilots, Aircraft Maintenance Engineers, Cabin Crew, Technicians and Ground Duty Service Officers. In 2003-04, India had only three domestic airlines with 123 commercial jets. But today, the scenario has changed.

In 2009 (till November) almost 40 million Indians took to the skies. It is estimated that by 2012, the airlines will add up a much larger fleet with a higher number of jobs. The Aviation sector has the potential of drawing $120 billion investments and creating 2-3 million jobs by 2020. So, if you want to fly like a bird, the Aviation sector paves path for your successful flight. The experts of the Aviation sector have estimated that the aviation jobs would grow at 35 per cent a year.

But 2009 airline passenger traffic posts biggest-ever fall in aviation history. The World airline passenger traffic fell 3.1 per cent, the biggest drop in aviation industry history, fuelled by the global financial down-turn, the International Civil Aviation Organization said. Preliminary figures for airline travel this year showed that international traffic declined by about 3.9 per cent and domestic traffic by 1.8 per cent, despite sharp growth in some regions. Total passenger traffic—both domestic and international—fell in all regions except the Middle East, which posted 10 per cent growth. All other regions recorded negative growth, with Africa hardest hit at minus 9.6 per cent overall, the ICAO said. The 3.1 per cent drop in passenger traffic this year compared to 2008 was the largtest on record for the industry and "reflects the one per cent drop in the world gross domestic product for the year," the organisation said in a statement.

"The double-digit domestic passenger traffic growth in the emerging markets of Asia and Latin America, and the relative strong performance of low cost carriers in North America, Europe and Asia Pacific helped curtail the decline in total traffic." The ICAO predicted a moderate recovery of 3.3 per cent growth for the airline industry next year, in line with improving economic conditions around the world.

If a person has a scientific bent of mind, he can opt for a career as a Pilot, Aircraft Maintenance Engineer etc. and if a person is good at communication and interpersonal skills, she/he can consider a career as an Air Hostess or a Flight Steward. The airlines today emphasise Cabin Crew to be an all important management and service dispenser as they are the direct face not only of the airline but also that of the country that the airline belongs to.

★ ★ ★

2. Types of Airline Personnel

FOR understanding how Airlines function and coordinate their flight schedules at various airports the work can be divided into three different functional heads-Airlines Operations, Technical and Engineering Division, Commercial division.

Airline Operations Inflight: Pilot, co-pilot and the cabin crew consisting of air hostesses/ flight pursers are the main people in airline operations during flight.After the terrorist attack on World Trade Centre in the US an Air Marshal accompanies the crew on board every airplane. He is trained in terrorist attack management and security.

Technical and Engineering Division: The team which maintains air crafts has specialists in avionics, mechanical, aeronautical and electronics engineering. Every aircraft needs proper maintenance and overhauling before it is allowed to fly. The engineering division is responsible for ensuring that the air crafts are fit to fly.

Commercial Division: From booking of tickets, reception, check in counter operations to cargo handling every airline has a wide variety of jobs to perform in the service of the passengers. There are business managers, travel tourism management executives, finance, law professional s and graduates handling various passenger service jobs. Announcers, ticketing clerks, reservation clerks, cargo handling personnel all comprise the commercial operations within an airline.

The various personnels can be listed as under:

- Flight crew members – They include captain and first officer;
- Flight engineer – Older aircraft need these on board;
- Flight attendants – These include supervisor, pursers, assistants and hostesses;
- In-flight security personnel – Some airlines have them on board in domestic sectors of international flights.
- Ground staff – They are responsible for operations at airports. They include:

Avionics engineers— They are responsible for certifying the flight and aircraft maintenance management;
Aerospace engineers— They attend to airframe, power plant and electrical system maintenance;

- Flight dispatchers – They include baggage handlers;
- Ramp managers – They handle miscellanious aspects;
- Gate agents – They are assigned to handle boarding and head-count;
- Ticket agents – They are assigned to see check-in, boarding passes, luggage receipts, overweight, seat-allocation etc. Some can be on the counter outside the airport for walk-in passenger ticketing;
- Passenger service agents – These are airline lounge employees or those who handle special-need passengers and escorting VIP/CIP, etc;
- Airlines follow a corporate structure where crew operations, maintenance, repairs, flight operation, passenger service etc. are supervised by a vice-president;
- Larger airlines often appoint VP's to oversee each of the airlines hubs as well. Lawyers' hubs deal with regulatory procedures and other administrative tasks. Human Resources is another critical division, which deals with security, trains and keeps stock of each employee's progress and leave record, medical pay, etc.

Factor Facilitators: The Factor Facilitators give training to the cockpit and cabin crew on resource management. They also undertake joint session of cabin crew, engineers and cockpit crew on working together.

Aviation Psychologists: The Aviation Psychologists assess the attitudes of the Pilots through psychometric tests. They also guide the young cabin crew to overcome the problems faced by them at their job.

Aviation Doctors: The Aviation Doctors conduct a rigorous medical check-up of the Pilots and other employees as per the norms of Aviation Medicine and the Central Medicine Establishment, both run by the Air Force. The airlines have to look their slots months in advance due to high rush of employees from different airlines.

★ ★ ★

3. The Cabin Crew

ABOUT THE JOB

Cabin crew is also known as flight attendants, airhostess or trolley dolly's. They are personnel on board the aircraft for the safety and welfare of passengers. If there were no services of food or drink during a flight, there would still have to be a minimum reserve of cabin crew for safety, as this is a legal requirement.

Because cabin crew members are the face of the airline, they are expected to explain services on board and always be enthusiastic, approachable and attractively presentable. Also role of the cabin crew can be physically demanding. You must be flexible to work any day of the year. This does, however, provide you perfect opportunities to get away from the repetitiveness of a normal 9 to 5 job! The crew encounter a variety of situations and have to be excellent team-players, with the innate ability of using their own quick thinking and organisational skills. Their position is one of stature and immense responsibility. They have to ensure a pleasant flying experience to create loyal customers.

While operating as a crew member, you may be required to perform the following duties or tasks during a flight:

- Conduct in-flight cabin crew services and serve prepared meals, beverage and other things;
- Greet passengers, supervise boarding and seating;
- Advise safety regulations, with demonstrations and announcements;
- Distribute reading material;
- Provide for seniors and assist sick passengers;
- Anticipate and provide for comfort of passengers needing special attention, including unaccompanied minors, parents with infants, disabled and elderly;
- Take extra care in the event of decompression, turbulence, mechanical malfunction, or unlawful acts by passengers.

Cabin crew are required to work in shifts, which are unsociable hours, working weekends and public holidays. They have to deal with differences in culture, ethnicity, food habits, climates, etiquettes and so on and so forth.

Depending on the routes they fly, cabin crew may get to do a lot of sightseeing, the longer the route the higher are the changes of sightseeing as the crews often change planes at 'slip point' or step overs. At these times they stay at luxury hotels at the airlines' expense.

DESIRABLE PERSONALITY TRAITS

A sense of responsibility and ability to handle crisis with intuition, a helpful and friendly approach with physical stamina and capacity are a must. Quickness in service and being effective and systematic is a requirement. An attractive personality and a well-modulated pleasant voice, a proportionate figure, with a positive attitude and bearing are some of the important points for service industry aspirants.

Communication skill cannot be underestimated; ability to deliver services in a relaxed and refined manner is a critical attribute. The ability to relate to people from different cultures is a key requisite. Being tactful yet active, enjoying teamwork and quick to react to a customer's need, are also necessary attributes.

Airlines prefer graduates, with a valid passport, preferably knowing foreign languages, if possible.

WORK ENVIRONMENT, SALARY AND BENEFITS

This is only a guide as each Airline has its own specific contracts, salary structure and benefits it offers.

They offer contracts which can be for one year or permanent, depending on clearing probationary competition tests. Medical fitness is mandatory.

Salary: Initially in domestic airlines, it can be up to 1.5 lakhs p.a. on confirmation and with increasing seniority, it can go up to 6 lakhs and more, including flight pay. What a crew member gets paid for can be a number of different elements.

- **Overnight Allowance:** If crew are required to spend the night away from the base, in addition to free 4/5 star hotel accommodation, transportation to and fro from airport;
- **Language Allowance:** If more than one foreign language are known;
- **Commission:** For selling duty-free items inflight;
- **Uniform Allowance:** Some airlines deduct monthly a fixed amount towards uniform given at the time of joining;
- **Laundry Allowance:** To maintain uniform according to company standards;
- **Meal Allowance:** Fixed amount paid towards missed meals on duty.

Benefits

- Reduced or free flight costs for crew and family;
- Private pension service;
- Holiday entitlement;

- Life insurance benefits;
- Medical care.

In addition, you can bid for flights on seniority and enjoy coordinated holidays or special days, i.e., anniversaries and birthdays, in different parts of the world.

IN A NUTSHELL

WHAT'S IT ABOUT?

An airhostess's primary job is to ensure the safety and security of passengers and she is specially trained and certified for safety and first-aid situations. She also has the added responsibility of making every passenger's flight comfortable in terms of customer service. Her tasks involve welcoming passengers on board, providing in-flight information, demonstrating emergency safety regulations and assisting old and sick passengers. An airhostess is expected to help passengers during critical situations calmly and patiently. There have been instances of airhostesses displaying exemplary courage and even laying down their lives for th sake of their passengers. It is an airhostess's responsibility to evacuate passengers from the plane during an emergency.

THE PAYOFF

An airhostess is paid according to her experience and the airline she works for. A fresher may earn Rs. 20,000-25,000 per month. A head flight attendant can earn up to Rs. 60,000 per month. Major international airlines pay Rs. 80,000 pm to Rs. 1 lakh per month. This can differ from organisation to organisation, and the number of hours one clocks per month.

SKILLS

- ✦ Ability to remain pleasant and presentable no matter how much the pressure.
- ✦ One has to stay fit. Good skin and good eyesight are musts.
- ✦ Functioning as a team player.
- ✦ Handling difficult situations and the ability to deal with them independently.

HOW DO I GET THERE?

The minimum qualification required is 10+2. It pays to be a graduate in any field or in hotel management. Knowledge of foreign language is a plus. Some airhostess training academies help you learn the ropes.

PROS & CONS

- ✦ Improves people management skills and self-confidence.
- ✦ One gets to explore the world.
- ✦ A well-paying job.
- ✦ Crazy hours, and some amount of menial work on-flight.
- ✦ Family life suffers.

A TYPICAL WORK DAY AND CABIN CREW

3.30 a.m.: Alarm for wake-up for rostered flight to Dubai. Put on make-up and uniform to look fresh and immaculate. Await your transportation for pick-up and report to Briefing Room at the Airport.

4.30 a.m.: Check your manual to refresh yourself with emergency equipment location and operation, for the aircraft you are operating on.

4.45 a.m.: Briefing with supervisor and other crew members for flight details, order of services, work zone and any special responsibilities for that particular flight, any special-need passenger under your care, ie, VIP/CIP to give attention to. They should also be prepared to be asked questions regarding safety and emergency procedures. After grooming check and breathalyzer test (at supervisor's discretion) they are introduced to captain, co-pilot, engineer and then proceed to clear customs and immigration formalities. Then proceed to the aircraft in crew transport.

5.10 a.m.: It's now time to prepare the aircraft before passengers board. Check safety equipment. Ensure that supplies are adequate. Make sure the cabin, toilets, and galleys are clean. Also conduct other regular checks for audio-visual systems, stocking up on reading material and immigration cards, put in safety instruction cards in every pocket with airsickness bag. Count and put out pillows and blankets on every seat.

Most importantly, check that required number of meals and special requests are uplifted, dry stores are stocked, prepare welcome drink trays. Check demo kit, make announcements ready after gathering information and plan for their order of delivery.

5.45 a.m.: Now, quickly refresh yourself and get into your position to help board and seat passengers, stowing luggage and helping with overcoats or large items.

6.10 a.m.: All the passengers are now seated, the aircraft is preparing to taxi on the runway. All the passengers view and hear safety procedures. They are also given demo to operate emergency exits. Ensure all passengers are seated, as are cabin crew for take-off.

6.20 a.m.: The services commence, once the seat belt sign is switched off, as per service procedures. Typical services offered are:-

- ❑ Headsets for inhouse entertainment;
- ❑ Drinks service;
- ❑ Meal service;
- ❑ Tea or coffee;
- ❑ Cold towel to refresh post-meal;
- ❑ Clearing of meal trays and cabin area;
- ❑ Selling duty-free items;
- ❑ Distributing disembarkation and immigration cards;
- ❑ Preparing cabin for landing;
- ❑ Periodic check on toilet cleaning, restocking supplies, dealing with queries or maintaining the safety and security of all the boarded passengers;
- ❑ Preparing for landing, bidding goodbye and returning items stored to passengers.

9.50 a.m.: Checking aircraft for any left items, restocking flight for the return journey and getting the cabin cleared up. Checking catering for aircraft meals according to passenger requests, cleaning out seat pockets and preparing for take-off procedures is to be done once again.

10.30 a.m.: Passengers start boarding for return sector Dubai-to-Delhi.

2.15 p.m.: Arrival Delhi, regular in-flight services. Cabin de-briefing to be done, also file in in-flight report and bar sales report. Go to pick-up point and take a drop home.

3.30 p.m.: Arrive home to catch some rest before next rostered flight.

★ ★ ★

4. Recruitment of Cabin Crew by NACIL

NATIONAL Aviation Company of India Limited (NACIL), which is a amalgamation of Indian Airlines and Air India Limited invites applications from Indian nationals (unmarried male and female) for the post of Cabin Crew, whenever vacancies exist.

ELIGIBILITY CRETERIA

The candidates must be between 18 and 25 years (relaxation as per rules).

Educational Qualification requirements are: Graduate from a recognized University. *OR* 10+2 with three years Diploma/Degree in Hotel Management & Catering Technology from a Government recognized Institute. *OR* 10+2 with minimum two years experience in the Service/ Hospitality industry*.

*For experience in Service/Hospitality industry, the following areas will be treated as relevant for determining eligibility:

- Airline/Aviation industry
- Call Centre/BPO
- Hotel Industry (minimum 3 Star)
- Event Management/Advertising Industry)
- Financial Sector (Banking/Insurance Companies)
- Travel & Tourism Agency (must be an IATA member)
- Reputed luxury & fashion goods retail/large retail chains
- Reputed Food/Coffee chains/specialty restaurant
- Healthcare
- Telecom
- Media

Candidates appearing in the final year examination in the year (of recruitment) of graduation or 3 years' diploma/degree in hotel management & catering technology can also apply provided they are able to produce their final years' result by specified date. If required, separate panels is formed for such candidates.

MEDICAL/PHYSICAL STANDARDS

The candidates must satisfy the physical standards that are specified.

Vision: Normal eyesight without glasses OR Corrected with contact lenses (Power of Lenses should not exceed ± 4D). Candidates who use glasses are not eligible to apply.

Colour Vision: Normal on Ishihara Plates.

(i) The clinical test done to check the Colour Vision deficiency of an individual is called "The Ishihara Colour Test". It is a test to diagnose colour deficiency.

(ii) "Colour Vision deficiency" or "Colour Blindness" is a condition in which certain colours cannot be distinguished, and is most commonly due to an inherited condition or in other words, it is the inability to perceive differences between some of the colours that other people can distinguish. It is most often of genetic nature.

Height & Weight: *Female:* Minimum 154.5 cms with proportionate weight.
Male: Minimum 163 cms with proportionate weight.
(For SC/ST candidates, minimum height is relaxable by 2.5 cms)

LANGUAGE

Fluency in English and one or more Indian Languages. Should also have working knowledge of Hindi. A candidate shall be deemed to have acquired working knowledge of Hindi, if he/she has passed:

(i) Matriculation or an equivalent or higher examination with Hindi as one of the subject; OR

(ii) Pragya, the examination conducted under Hindi Teaching Scheme of the Central Government or when so specified by that Government in respect of any particular category of post, any lower examination under that scheme; OR

(iii) Any other examinaton specified on that behalf by the Central Government; OR

(iv) He/she declares himself/herself to have acquired such knowledge.

SELECTION PROCEDURE

Eligible candidates would be required to go through Group Dynamics & Personality Assessment Test (GD & PAT) at the venues as decided by National Aviation Company of India Limited. GD & PAT shall be conducted in phases. Candidates who qualify the same will appear for personal interview.

Weightage for experience: Candidates with graduation Degree or 3 years Diploma in Hotel Management & Catering Technology will be given due weightage of experience of minimum one year, after obtaining the requisite academic qualification, in the following:

(i) Airport handling/Customer Services or as a Cabin Crew in an Airline; OR

(ii) Front Office/Guest Relations or as a Restaurant Hostess/Steward in a 5 Star Hotel.

Candidates with 10+2 qualification only, will be assigned weightage for having experience in the above areas beyond the minimum requirement of 2 years.

★ ★ ★

5. Training Avenues for Prospective Cabin Crew

THE AVENUES

1. **E-learning Courses:** These are available on internet, which is a way popular and easily accessible to today's generation. Normally, a certificate is awarded at the completion of the modules. There are tests to self-evaluation as well. These courses offer the advantage of learning at your own place and time. Most offer only the theoretical knowledge about topics that are commonly touched upon. This conforms to standard DGCA guidelines about basic training needed for flying crew. They can be paid for and enrolled for online. Tests and results are conducted online. However, no practical skills are imparted or interviews arranged. These courses are, therefore, very reasonably priced, as compared to professional training institutes. But there is no guarantee of a career after completion of the course. Candidates have to pursue the available opportunities independently.

2. **Professional Training Institutes:** These have mushroomed in the last 5 years and are very popular with the young aspirants, who see them as a stepping stage to a flying career. The courses offered are generally of 1-year duration, with a diploma awarded on completion. Most offer an international affiliation with an established university, or are validated by a well-known authority to give an international acceptance. The curriculum is based on DGCA-approved topics like first aid, swimming, grooming, persona enhancement, and travel and tourism orientation. Even a short stint of reservation and computerised booking systems being used today, are included. Most importantly, perfecting communication skills and social etiquettes is practised. The advertisements for these institutes are very prominent in magazines and hoardings, so they harvest a large catch and annually, there are a good number of freshers looking for opportunities in this industry. These institutes have made their presence felt in the regional and interior areas, being centrally located, besides, the smart designer uniforms. The USP is the placement if not a guarantee of job at the completion of the course, which is a definite magnet pull for all aspirants. Parents too find the deal convenient as fees are considered as "settlement amount" for a service job 12 months down the line. Another

major plus is that a candidate is seen as having made a commitment to researching these career options. Airlines have a fast track scheme to differentiate between trained students and other candidates.

Certain points must be observed in choosing the right training avenue. Claims and figures must be verified before enrolment. The dynamics of economy also affect the industry adversely. There are cycles of highs and lows in every field, which must be considered. That also govern the employment scene not only in India, but globally.

3. **Employment Agencies:** These recruit prospective candidates, whose data is available either online or in person. Often a commission is levied for services rendered like arranging an interview or a portion of the salary is taken on selection. The individuals are briefed about the job and company culture. Guidelines are shared about work culture, salary structure, job specifics, hierarchy, etc.

4. **Direct Recruitment:** Airlines advertise in dailies, when vacancies arise. All basics are mentioned for the specific post. Most airlines and hotels accept online applications, but the process is more personalised today. The walk-in screening interviews are held for the initial round, followed by a personal round in medicals and a group dynamics session.

The procedure is very exhilarating, atmosphere-competitive and end-rewarding. The numbers for such interviews run into thousands on the day they are conducted and the shortlisted feel like they are on the moon. Thus, these vacancies are eagerly awaited and such evergreen jobs will never have dearth of applicants. This is the best short cut for a long-awaited career.

VARIOUS INSTITUTES OFFERING TRAINING

1. **Aviation Academy:** This is an APTECH Ltd. Initiators are offered, cabin crew and airport ground staff training, airport management as well as personality development and ticketing. *(www.aviationacademy.net)*, *(www.theaviationacademy.co.uk)*
2. **Acumen Institute:** It has an exclusive tie-up with Halifax College, London for an international certificate, with exciting offers like free housing in Singapore with no extra cost and so on. They offer aviation management certificate in 6 months as well as a certification programme in interviews orientation and aviation grooming in 3 months. They also offer international diploma in hospitality and travel management. *(www.acumeninstitute.org)*, *(www.acumeneducation.in)*, *(www.acumen.vic.edu.au)*
3. **Airhostess Academy:** Since 1997, it is the pioneer in training students for airhostess/purser/airport ground staff. Duration of course is either 1 year or two years. *(www.airhostessacademy.com)*.
4. **Cabin Crew Academy:** They offer a diploma in aviation and travel management.

5. **Flying Cats:** It is a complete school, awarding a BBA in aviation, along with Annamalai University.
6. **Frankfinn:** It offers a coordinated certificate from Jet Airways with a diploma. *(www.frankfinn.com)*
7. **Vertex Aviation Academy:** It offers a diploma in hospitality management.
8. **Career Zone:** It has been training airhostesses since 1984, awarding a diploma in aviation and hospitality management. *(www.nycareerzone.org)*
9. **Kuoni Academy:** Kuoni Academy Co. Inc has joined hands with Cabin Crew Career (UK). It provides intensive training in key areas and interview guidance. It also has many centres all over India and is well-established. *(www.kuoniacademy.co.in)*
10. **Kingfisher Academy:** (careerenquiry@kingfisheracademy.com). The airline has floated its own training institute offering only placement assistance, not mandatory absorption. *(www.kingfisheracademy.com)*
11. **IABA:** IABA Airhostess Training Centre, Dwarka, New Delhi. *(www.IABA.in)*

Besides, there are many more institutes spreading all over the country, which provide certificates and diplomas in various areas of aviation. EBS Aviation Training, Maples Institute of Airhostess Training and Centre for Civil Aviation Training are to name a few.

★ ★ ★

6. Basic Requirements for Flight Attendant

If you have ever considered the list of basic flight attendant requirements, you may have questioned some of them as they refer to you. In an attempt to clarify and simplify, some of these will be explained in more detail here, starting with the basics.

As a flight attendant applicant, you must be a high school graduate; if you do not have a diploma, a Government Equivalent Degree (GED) is sufficient. A college degree is not required, but you must have at least 2 years of college or 2 years' experience working with the public. Airlines like to see stability—proof that you can finish things that you start is important when an airline is considering you for employment. They are also interested in any jobs you have had which show you are able to work well with the public.

You must have a clean background. Airlines perform a 10-year background check, so it is important that your resume does not contain any gaps. For security purposes, they need to know where you have been for the past decade, that you can account for your whereabouts. If you have a gap in which you were raising children as a stay-at-home mom or you were travelling for an extended period of time without employment, you will need to get a friend or acquaintance who can write a statement to vouch for your activities during that time. Included in the background check are drug screens; be aware that some substances can remain in the body for 30 days or more, and airlines are a no-tolerance industry when it comes to illegal drug usage.

When applying to an airline, it is imperative that you have a valid passport. Most airlines now will not even interview you if you do not have a passport in your hand, even if that airline does not have international routes. The reason for that is, you could find yourself in a situation where you are involuntarily diverted to another country during flight. In some countries, you can find it difficult to get home or even seek contact with your homeland if you can't prove your citizenship.

You must have an acceptable range of vision to work as a flight attendant. Vision must be correctable to 20/40 or better. Should you encounter an emergency situation, it is especially critical that you have good eyesight, as you will be better equipped to cope with any difficult conditions that may arise.

Airlines require you to be at least 18 years of age. Most require age 20 as a minimum, but several airlines accept 18- and 19-year-olds. Stressful situations may occur in-flight, and naturally, the more life experience you have had, the better your ability to handle the situation. Maturity and reliability are important attributes to airlines. Episodes such as inebriated customers, difficult personalities, medical problems and in-flight irregularities may transpire, and younger applicants can lack the skills necessary to deal with these unpredictable circumstances.

Airlines typically carry customers from points all over the globe, from all walks of life. While they welcome diversity in employees and truly need employees who can relate to people of diverse cultures. U.S. airlines require their employees to possess a good command of the English Language. Airlines very much appreciate bilingual employees, but they must be able to be easily understood by customers for the express purpose of being able to direct customers effectively during an emergency. Things happen quickly during crises, and flight crews must be able to communicate clearly and accurately.

Finally, airlines like to hire people who pleasingly project their company image. Beauty is not a prerequisite, but employees do need to be well-groomed and professional, with a positive attitude and pleasing personality. Flexibility is mandatory, and weight should be in proportion to height. The weight requirement is not so much for aesthetic reasons as it is a safety issue. A flight attendant must be able to fit comfortably on a very narrow jumpseat, seated alongside another flight attendant; be able to move easily down aisles that have become increasingly narrower, and be able to exit the small window exit openings. Flight attendants must be physically fit enough to work extended hours, lift at least 50 pounds, work while standing for prolonged periods, and deal with fluctuating schedules and working conditions. Being a flight attendant is a hard work, and not a job for the faint of heart, but if you meet these requirements, you can be on your way to a fun career in the skies.

★ ★ ★

7. What the Recruiter Won't Tell You

There are many guidelines out there nowadays to instruct the flight attendant candidate on how to apply for an airline job. But few will tell you some of the underlying truths about why some do not get hired.

Many variables enter into the recruitment equation. It is not only a matter of how well you answer questions or how classy the clothes you wear to the interview. True professionalism requires forethought, planning and basic common sense. In order to project a refined appearance, it is important to remember the "little things" that can keep you apart from the rest and hold you back in your pursuit of your goal.

Aside from the usual requirements, there are things that you need to know about flight attendant interviews that no one will tell you. It is acceptable to apply if you have less than perfect vision or a little bit of an overbite, but if your teeth are exceptionally crooked, yellow or out of alignment, this may be looked upon unfavourably.

Airlines consider the flight attendant to be along the front lines in conveying the corporate image. There is nothing that is more of a turn-off than someone who is very obviously in need of dental care, and it is imperative to choose people who possess a healthy and polished image.

Have your teeth cleaned prior to going to the interview and consult your dentist about any necessary cosmetic dentistry you may need, such as repairing any noticeable gaps or missing teeth. If you need your teeth to be capped or bonded and have been putting it off, now is the time to do it.

Another item that is often overlooked is the scar. If you have a small but noticeable scar on your face, hands or arms, it is not necessary to worry—few of us have baby-perfect skin. But if you have a larger or more obvious one, a cosmetic course of action may be in order. Try applying Dermablend to the scar. This product is what beauty pageant contestants use to cover imperfections, as it is an excellent concealer, and can be purchased at any major department store. If the scar is distractingly obvious, you may want to invest in some cosmetic surgery to improve your look. This is particularly important if you are interested in a flight attendant or any other customer service type of position where you are in the limelight.

Many people speak with an accent, whether it is a southern, northern, western, eastern or a foreign one, and many times there are cultural differences in how we express ourselves. This, in itself, usually poses no problem. But the incorrect pronunciation of words or use of poor grammar will detract your professional image and lessen your chances of consideration for employment as a flight attendant.

No matter how impeccably a flight attendant candidate is dressed, it can make a recruiter's skin crawl to hear double negatives, slang words, cursing, mispronounced words or other such undignified grammatical errors. This is the business world, and such indiscretions are not acceptable. Brush up on your speaking skills—take a class in public speaking or ask a teacher or an articulate friend to help you if you have trouble.

Many airlines require flight attendant applicants to read a boarding card during the interview, to ensure that they have adequate verbal skills, so make it a habit to practise using correct speech in your daily life. If you have an obvious speech defect or a shrill, weak, monotone or otherwise annoying voice, this will also distract from your presentation.

Working with a speech therapist will improve a voice problem or speech defect and help you to overcome the problem. All these things can interfere with your professional life in the workplace. An unprofessional resume with obvious gaps or one that indicates an excess of "job-hopping" will not win you points with recruiters. Do your homework. If you don't know how to construct a resume, get help from a professional. It's not brain surgery, but there are things you need to include and certain ways to best showcase your experience.

If your hair need colouring, do it before the interview. Brassy, unnatural colours and roots that are showing are also bad news. Consult a colourist if you have difficulty managing your hairstyle or colour. There is no excuse for telltale roots or a bad hairdo ruining your looks, especially since it is so easily fixed. If you leave something like this undone, it says to the interviewer that you don't care enough to bother. Big problem, easy solution. Enough said.

Check yourself in a mirror before you go for an interview. There is no reason why you would enter this type of situation with food between your teeth, a mascara smudge on your cheek, a slip that shows or lipstick on your teeth, so take a quick peek in the mirror first.

Airlines really do consider how their image is perceived to the flying public. If an employee's persona detracts from that of company's image, the company will not be interested in having that person represent them to the public. Doing what it takes to get ahead in the business world will not only land you the job of a lifetime, but will give you a more confident and self-assured outlook on the future.

★ ★ ★

8. Interview and Selection Procedures

THE candidates either have a walk-in short listing or are called for an introductory round where CVs are scrutinised and a brief interaction happens between designated airline employees and aspirants.

Sometimes height and weight are also checked for airlines requirements. A GD may be scheduled later in the day. You are assessed on given parameters and will be asked to appear for a final interview on another day.

The final interview is done to determine that you are the right person for the job and you will be informed, if selected, to go for a medical test. Once you're successful in meeting the requisite standards demanded, you will be given an offer, the training will be held at centres of the airline, lasting for 2-3 months. Accommodation is provided only for initial week, but assistance is given to locate and share space.

Once training is complete, testing is done and certificates awarded with results, you are then placed on probation for a while, where you assist cabin crew on flights. You will then operate independently till you are confirmed by 6 months and then, it's your life, as you planned it!

CABIN CREW—SOME FAQ'S

1. **I cannot speak another language. Is this going to stop me from applying for the job of a cabin crew?**

   Knowledge of another language or more is desirable, but not essential for becoming crew.

2. **I am not a graduate. Will this hinder my selection?**

   Today, most airlines want a well-rounded individual, aware and articulate and graduates are preferred. But if you have previous experience in customer services, you will still be considered. If you have completed a course in cabin crew training, it will be a distinct advantage and you will be considered seriously for your commitment.

3. **How much salary will I get as cabin crew?**

   Most domestic airlines pay Rs. 10,000 initially and increase up to 28,000/- pm as seniority increases. Allowances are paid for missed meals, overtime, day allowances, laundry etc. in addition. The perks add up to quite an amount by way of free medical, stopovers, tickets over the airlines network etc.

4. **I'm married and have children; does this affect my chances of becoming a cabin crew?**

   Many cabin crews are married and have families. In India, airlines prefer you to be unmarried at the time of selection though.

5. **Can I apply for more than one region?**

   No. You can apply only for one region posted. In case you apply for more than one region, you will not be considered at all.

6. **How should I apply, through post or in person?**

   Only Ex-services or those employed in Govt./semi Govt./PSU can apply by post. Other candidates can do online application.

7. **What do I need to have before applying online?**

   (a) A valid email id for communication;
   (b) Drafts of DD for Rs. .../- (not for SC/ST candidates). (The fee may vary from airline-to-airline;
   (c) Exact height in cms (please refer to Ht and Wt chart);
   (d) Your exact wt in kgs;
   (e) Details of caste certificates: i.e. date of issue and issuing authority) for SC/ST/OBC candidates only;

8. **What is the selection procedure to go through?**

   Eligible candidates would go through Group dynamics and personality assessment tests (GD & PAT). Those who qualify will be required to appear for preliminary physical exam for Height/Weight. and vision conducted by the airline's medical officer and those who clear the interview will appear for a personal interview.

TEN TOUGH INTERVIEW QUESTIONS AND THEIR ANSWERS

Mental fear of the unknown is often which produces the physical symptoms of nervousness. In addition to preparing yourself physically, you need to prepare yourself mentally. The best way to prepare mentaliy is to know what may be coming. Facing the unknown can only exist when there is an unknown. Take the time to understand the "standards" when it comes to interviewing questions.

The following are some of the most difficult questions faced in the course of job interviews. Some questions may seem rather simple on the surface, such as 'Tell us about yourself'—but these questions can have a variety of answers. The more open-ended the question, the wider the variation in the answers. Once you have practised your interviewing skills, you will find that you can use almost any question as a launching pad for a particular topic or compelling story.

Others are classic interview questions, such as "what is your greatest weakness?'. Most people answer these questions improperly. In this case, the standard textbook reply to the "greatest weakness" question is to provide a veiled positive reply such as: "I work too much. I just work and work and work and work." Wrong. Either you are lying or, worse still you are telling the truth, in which case you define working too much as a weakness and you do not want to work much at all!

The following answers that are provided will give you a new perspective on how to feel your way though interview questions. They are not there for you to lift from the page and repeat for your next interview. They are provided for you to use as the basic structure in formulating your own answers. While the specifics of each reply may not apply to follow the basic structure of the question, answer from the perspective of the interview. Answer the questions behaviorally, with specific examples that clearly back up what you are saying about yourself. Always provide information that since you want to become the very best employee for the company and that you have specially prepared yourself to become exactly that. They want to be sold. They are waiting to be sold. Don't disappoint them!

1. **Tell me about yourself.**

   It seems like an easy interview question. It's open ended. I can tell whatever I want from the birth canal forward. Right?

   Wrong. What the hiring manager really wants is a quick, two to three snapshots of whom you are and why you are the best candidate for this position.

   So as you answer this question, talk about what you've done to prepare yourself to be the very best candidate for the position. Use an example or two. Then, ask if they would like more details. If they do, keep giving them examples of your background and experience. Always point back to the example when you have the opportunity.

   "Tell me about yourself" does not mean tell me everything. Just tell them what makes you the best.

2. **Why should I hire you? or**
   Are you the best person for the job? Show it by your passionate examples.

   The easy answer is that you are the best person for the job. And don't be afraid to say so. But then back it up with what specifically differentiates you. For example: "You should hire me because I'm the best person for the job. I realize that there are likely other candidates who also have the ability for this job. Yet I bring an additional quality that makes me the best person for my passion for excellence. I am passionately committed to producing top class results. For example..."

3. **What is your long-range objective?**

   (Make my job enhance me. Make me want to hire you.)

   The key is to focus on your achievable objectives and what you are doing about those objectives.

For example: "Within five years, I would like to become the very best asset your company has on staff. I want to work towards becoming the expert to rely upon. And in doing so, I feel I'll be fully prepared to take on any responsibilities which might be presented in the long-term. For example, what I'm presently doing to prepare myself...."Then go on to show by your examples what you are doing to reach your objectives.

4. **How has your education prepared you for your career?**

This is a broad question and you need to focus on the behavioral example of educational background which specifically aligns to the required field you are competing for in your chosen career.

An example: "My education has focused on not only the learning, the fund but also on the practical application of the information learned within those. For example, I played a lead role in a class project where we gathered and analyzed best practice data from this industry. Let me tell you more about the results..."

Focus on behavioral examples supporting the key competencies for them. Then, ask if they would like to hear more examples.

5. **Are you a team player?**

Almost everyone says yes to these questions. But it is not just a yes/no question. You need to provide behavioral examples to back up your answer.

A sample answer: "Yes, I'm very much a team player. In fact, I had plenty of opportunities in my work, school and athletics to develop my skills as a player. For example, on a recent project..."

Emphasize teamwork behavioral examples and focus on your openness to people of backgrounds. Talk about the strength of the team above the Individual. This question may be used as a lead into questions around how you conflict within a team, so be prepared.

6. **Have you ever had a conflict with a boss or professor? How was it resolved?**

Note that if you says no, most interviewers will keep drilling deeper conflict. The key is how you behaviorally reacted to conflict and what you did to resolve it.

For example: "Yes, I have had conflicts in the past. Never major ones. There have been disagreements that needed to be resolved. I've found that when that occurs, it helps to fully understand the other person's perspective, so I talk, listen to their point of view, and then I seek to work out a collaborative solution. For example..."

Focus your answer on the behavioral process for resolving the conflict collaboratively.

7. **What is your greatest weakness?**

Most career books tell you to select strength and present it as a weakness as: "I work too much. I just work and work and work." Wrong. First of all, it is a strength and presenting it as a weakness is deceiving. Second, it misses the crux of the question.

You should select a weakness that you have been actively working to improve on. For example: "I have had trouble in the past with planning and pricing. However, I'm now taking steps to correct this. I just started using planner..." then show them your planner and how you are using it.

Talk about a true weakness and show what you are doing to overcome it.

8. If I were to ask your professors to describe you, what would they say?

This is a threat of reference check question. Do not wait for the interview to be over for the answer. Ask any prior bosses or professors in advance. And if they provide a positive reference, ask them for a letter of recommendation.

Then you can answer the question like this:

"I believe she would say I'm a very energetic person, that I'm results-oriented; one of the best people she has ever worked with. Actually, I know she said that, because those are her very words. May I show you her recommendation?"

So be prepared in advance with your letters of recommendation.

9. What qualities do you feel a successful manager should have?

Focus on two words: leadership and vision.

Here is a sample of how to respond: "The key quality in a successful manager is divided into two. It should be leadership and the ability to be the visionary for the people who are under them. The person who can set the course and direction for subordinates in the highest calling of a true leader in inspiring others to manage to reach the highest abilities. I'd like to tell you about a person whom I consider to be a true leader.

Then, give an example of someone who has touched your life and how they have helped in your personal development.

10. If you had to live your life over again, what one thing would you change?

Focus on a key turning point in your life or missed opportunity. Yet you look forward to what you are doing, to still seek to make that change.

For example: "Although I'm overall very happy with where I'm right now, one aspect I likely would have changed if I had focused earlier on another career. I had a great internship this past year and look forward to more experience in the field. I simply wish I would have focused here earlier. For example, on my recent internship..." ... then provide examples.

Stay focused on the positive direction in your life and back it up with examples.

In reviewing these responses, please remember that they are only to be viewed. Please do not rehearse them verbatim or adopt them as your own. They are merely your creative juices to get you thinking about how to properly answer the range of questions that you may face.

SOME CRUCIAL QUESTIONS

When attending a flight attendant job interview, what are the proper responses to these questions?

Tell me why I should select you.

Why do you want to be a flight attendant?

Why do you want to work for this airline?

Answer:

When you are put forth a question such as "Tell me why I should select you", it is your job to give a persuasive answer to hire you based on your qualifications. Blow your own trumpet—this is a chance to sell yourself to the company. Give them a good reason to hire your services—impress upon them how reliable, punctual, flexible you are, how you are able to anticipate the needs of others, an essential requirement of any customer service job. Communicate how your positive contributions and performance at your present job will relate to that of the flight attendant position.

When asked "Why do you want to be a flight attendant?" be different and creative. Do NOT say that oft-repeated run of the mill answer like you want to travel and you like to meet people—that's the most common answer, and they would have heard that hundreds of times a day! Give an answer that implies that you enjoy giving good customer service, or that it's like going to work every day and feeling like you're on vacation; emphasise your passion for aeroplanes and flying since that is what you will be actually doing in a flight attendant job, and be creative with your answer. Really dig into what it is that appeals to you about the job, and think about what it is that charms you to the position.

For the question "Why do you want to work for this airline?" you first need to know and establish the fact that you already know something about the airline. Go to their website and learn several facts about them, such as any new routes they may be planning, if they have ordered any new aeroplanes, how many flight attendants they plan to hire this year, or changes in management such as the name of their new Operations Manager or CEO. Then you want to convince them what difference you could bring to their company, giving specific examples of the ways how the company has already impacted your life or how it will in the future. Keep in mind that this is your big chance to persuade them to hire you, so learn all you can about how your background will help you fit into their company's culture, and don't be afraid to brag on your accomplishments and assets.

Flight attendant interview skills are no different from general interview tackling skills. Like developing any skill, solid interviewing skills are developed through repetition and evaluation.

The following practice techniques are effective and proven ways to prepare for your interviews.

Live Session: By far, the best and the most economical way to practise interviewing is to have a friend or family member to conduct mock interview sessions. The mock interview sessions should be set up in a part of your home to exactly replicate the interviewing environment—perhaps an office with a desk, so you can incorporate as much realism as possible into the interview practice session. The "interviewer" should ask you the questions provided in the Interview Questions section and critique your responses, body language, etc. If you are preparing for an open interview, practise your answers in front of a large group of friends or family members and ask for their feedback.

Tape-recorded Session: Using an audio cassette recorder has numerous advantages like; you do not need anyone else to help you. You can dictate your responses to each question and then play them back for analysis. Be particularly attentive to your use of what we call "useless words," such as "You know," "Ya know," "like," etc. These words have no place in an interview setting. You can also try to record the interview with a friend asking the questions. Here again, you can benefit from someone else's feedback.

Videotaped Session: This is the most effective form of interview practice that is used by many employment consulting firms, but if you own a camcorder, you can achieve the same results for a lot less money. To be most effective, you should have another individual acting as the interviewer. You should create an interview "set" and go through all the motions you would during an actual interview, from the introduction to the final handshake. The results of your videotaped interview can be very surprising. Very often, you will notice personal negative habits that you were perhaps never aware of. You should repeatedly tape the session until you are satisfied with your performance. Then, the actual interview should be a lot easier.

Below given are few of the details that one should be aware of before attending the flight attendant interview as it will help you immensely during the interview process. The more you know about a specific company, the more prepared you will be to not only answer the interviewer's questions, but you will be able to ask your own, equally intelligent, questions.

Knowing the answers to these questions will give you a competitive advantage over fellow applicants.

- ***Which category does the airline belong to?***
- ***What is the airline's position vis-à-vis its competitors?***
- ***What are the names of the senior management team?***
- ***What was the airline's total annual operating revenue for the previous year?***
- ***How much was the airline's growth rate with respect to revenue?***
- ***What is the airline's employee growth rate?***
- ***How many employees does the airline have?***
- ***How many flight attendants does the airline have?***
- ***What equipment does the airline fly?***
- ***What is the primary route structure?***
- ***How many destinations does the airline fly to?***
- ***What to Expect?***

Given below is information on what to expect at various airline open house interviews for an air hostess job. Here, we will discuss current practices at a typical open house interview, although format may vary by airline.

The open house interview (also called open interview session or job fair) is a general information session for you and gives the airline a chance to screen a large group of potential candidates at one location. Sessions are scheduled after successful completion of an online pre-screening (invited) or may be open to anyone (uninvited). Open house dates are usually published on the airline's website.

There is normally a morning and afternoon session. If there is a choice, I recommend scheduling the morning session, since interviewers are freshest and friendliest in the morning. At the open interview session, typically you will be asked to fill out a questionnaire and will be given a short speech about the airline by a flight attendant representative. Each person may then be required to take a written, multiple-choice test, which includes some customer service questions. Those that pass the test will be asked to remain while the others are excused. The remaining group will be asked to speak or read in front of the group. Usually, the topic deals in some way with customer service. Resumes or applications are usually not collected at the open house. Most successful candidates are advised during this session of their advancement to a second interview, although airlines have also been advising some candidates by mail. There are sometimes individual interviews at the open house session.

SOME OTHER CRITICAL QUESTIONS

Below are given same sample questions, these are regularly asked to assess core values skills in the final round. It's advised to prepare appropriate replies so that the replies can be the deciding factor in your favour.

(a) *Competency check*

1. What do you do on an ongoing basis to update yourself professionally?
2. What are key competencies required in your current assignment?

(b) *Respect for social resources*

1. What kind of experience do you have in budgetary responsibility and have you kept within that?
2. Can you tell us how you maximize the benefit produced from the limited resources you were given?

(c) *Integrity*

1. How did you confront someone or give a candid feedback to in your office?
2. Were you loyal to your co-workers or to your company?

(d) *Team work*

1. What do you do as a member/leader to address an ongoing office problem?
2. Tell us how you disguised with objectives of a team and how you handled it?

(e) Exceeding customer expectation

1. How do you gather and use feedback from customers?
2. Tell us about a time you "wowed" a customer.

(f) Respect for others

1. How do you handle differences arising from different backgrounds of people at work?
2. Do you encourage people to express their ideas and aspirations? Give an example.

(g) Innovation

1. How do you implement an idea of yours at work?
2. How different and welcomed is your initiative by others?

(h) Accountability

1. How do you report progress at work?
2. How do you follow up on projects you delegate to others?

(i) Customer service

1. Prescribe your moot rewarding public dealing experience.
2. How will you handle a customer who wants priority, when you are working at a deadline for a project?

(j) Ability to handle pressure

1. Describe an incident, where you did not handle pressure well.
2. What flusters you more, lots of work or no work?

(k) Ability to supervise

1. What would your colleagues say about you as a co-worker?
2. Which skills are you better at leading or following?

(l) Accuracy

1. Tell us about a job that required you to be accurate.
2. What do you do to control error?

(m) Dependable

1. Can we check with your office as to how many days you were late for work?
2. Are you known as a dependable individual?

(n) Detail-oriented

1. How do you fare at multi-tasking?
2. How do you keep track of work that needs constant attention?

(o) Handling complex problems

1. Describe how you think through a different problem.
2. Did you make any charges in the project you feel proud about?

(*p*) ***Power questions***

1. Tell us your greatest strength/weakness.
2. Do you call yourself a self-starter? Why?

(*q*) ***Office skills***

1. What constitutes office atmosphere—dress, rules, discipline?
2. When there is repetitive work, how do you handle boredom?

(*r*) ***Current/last job***

1. Who do you report to?
2. What is the most constant criticism you have faced?

(*s*) ***Work with supervision***

1. Would you rather be closely supervised and given good direction, or work out solutions for yourself?
2. What kind of recommendation will your superior give me about your ability to complete a given task satisfactorily?

OVERALL READINESS ASSESSMENT QUIZ

1. Have you planned your outfit and dealt with grooming?
2. Have you got your latest photograph, full face and in a western attire?
3. Have you got copies of your CV, references and recommendation letters as well as your educational certificates?
4. Have you looked at the website of the company you are approaching for an interview and familiarized yourself with pertinent details?
5. Have you updated yourself with latest news and current events?
6. Are you knowledgeable about the airlines culture, destinations, floor, hierarchy, salary structure etc.?
7. Have you prepared suitable replies to critical questions?
8. Are you prepared to be posted to another city if selected?
9. Do you know about any financial transactions required *i.e.*, bond/security monies that you may have to comply with?
10. Have you kept you options open about other jobs/careers?
11. What range of compensation are you seeking?
12. What is your projected career graph in your estimation?
13. Have you realistically evaluated your candidature with regard to the job's specifications?
14. How will you sell yourself to your prospective employees?
15. Have you worked out why they should choose you, above other similar aspirants?

TIPS TO HANDLE GD AND PI (Group Discussions and Personal Interview)

As no two individuals are similar, the airlines adopt standard procedures to assess candidates, who are capable of mature thinking and taking the initiative according to the situation.

1. One week before the GD, you must go through the current news/topics which is very helpful to pick up the right thought.
2. Make the right views related to the topic given and keep it in mind for right approach.
3. Even if starting the discussion bring you the notice of the examiner, it can be a plus point for you if you don't start the discussion first because this gives you the sufficient time to pickup the line.
4. Listen carefully the views of other's. Its better to be silent instead of giving a wrong statement.
5. Try to display original ideas and faced the challenge with assurance and determination.
6. Speak clearly revealing good command over the language. Make sure you are audible.
7. Always gives chance and support to others.
8. Don't loose your patience. Be calm.
9. Don't create controversies and quarrels with others.
10. Always gives your arguments logically and rationally giving emphasis on important points to clinch the issue.
11. Adopt a mature and scientific approach.
12. Be persuasive and convince others trying to win them over by way of thinking.
13. Don't be confused the timid. It shows your lack of confidence.
14. Don't be emotional or display unsteady behaviour.

Before appearing for the interview make sure you are well prepared so that you are relaxed at the time you walk in the door. Your winning resume has already given you entry to the potential recruiter. But do remember that it has also given some kind of information and impression about you on the interviewer. He has read your resume and is expected to ask questions based on the hard facts stated in your resume. The sure way to be successful in the interview is to be prepared.

★★★

9. Interview Preparation

GETTING PREPARED

I. Tell us about yourself

This is an open canvas for you, giving you an opportunity to direct and lead your interview in the direction you want. A good idea would be to structure your answer in the following broad heads:

- Name;
- Hometown;
- Family background;
- Educational background (starting from schooling to professional qualifications);
- Achievements;
- Hobbies.

In all the above subheads speak only that information which will give strength to your candidature. Avoid verbose description of yourself.

There could be a follow-up on this. Mention how your interest in that hobby can be used profitably in this job, for example, NSS made you adventurous, helped to accept challenges and face difficult situations. These incidents helped to add a dimension to your personality and are an asset you will carry with you to the organisation.

2. Why do you want to join us?

To answer this question, you need to research the company well. Here, you can quote some of your personal beliefs, which are in conjunction with the values of the company or talk about specific products and services which could be of interest to you too.

In the event where your skill set is mapping with the requirement of the company, do not miss the chance to highlight the same. Specify the initiatives taken or work done to attain that skill set.

3. What would you like to do in five years' time?

This question is asked to assess candidate's career plan and ambition for growth and to see if the company will be able to provide that opportunity over a period of time. Also to assess if your personal goals are not totally off tangent with what company's objectives are. It is also to check your stability with the organisation. It is a good idea to be very realistic in your answer. If required guidance should be taken from your seniors who are already in the corporate environment.

You can say you would be at a much senior post, with additional hands-on experience of the job and knowledge of the whole spectrum of jobs, rather than only the one you are interviewing for. You would be a team leader with independent control and responsibilities.

4. Do you prefer working with others or alone?

This question is usually asked to determine whether you are a team player. Before answering, however, be sure about the eligibility requirement of job profile, that whether it requires team work or you to work alone. Then answer accordingly.

5. What are your biggest accomplishments?

You could begin your reply with: "Although I feel my biggest achievements are still ahead of me, I am proud of my sense of involvement. I would like to make my contribution as part of that team and learn a lot in the process".

It will be a good idea to close your answer with also specifying what attributes and circumstances made you succeed.

6. What are your favourite subjects?

It is a leading question giving direction to the panel members for possible areas where they can probe in further for your knowledge base and in-depth understanding. It is advisable to select the topics that you are competent in.

7. Why should we hire you?

Keep your answer short and precise. You should highlight areas from your background that relates to the need of the organisation. Recap the organisation's description of the job, meeting it point by point with your skills.

Mention that you should be hired for your knowledge, skills, attitude, confidence level and your commitment towards the organisation.

8. What are your hobbies?

This question is generally asked to assess whether you are "desktop" kind of a person or an "interaction orientated person". It also indicates your preference for team-oriented activities or projects with solo contributions. It enables the organisation to place you accordingly after selection. Be candid in answering the questions.

You should emphasise on your extrovert nature, team player attitude, willingness to accept challenges and further skills; for example, if you sing, say I can do solo as well as a group performance, you can control the crowd during a performance and get them to participate.

9. What is the worst feedback you have ever got?

To answer this question, you must admit and share your areas of improvement. Also sharing an action plan for improving oneself will indicate your ability to take criticism well. Your answer should reflect your open-mindedness.

10. What is the most difficult situation you have faced?

Here, you should be ready with your real life story. The question looks for information on two fronts: How do you define difficulty and how did you handle the situation? You should be able to clearly lay down the road map for solving the problem, your ability to perform task management and maintain good interaction with your team members and other peers. It is advisable to close by highlighting the lesson learnt out of the incident.

11. How do you measure talent in an organisation, company or team? or (How do you grow or develop talent in an organisation or company or team)?

That's a very significant question. Its implications affect the future health of all organisations probably now more than ever.

The reason why this is such a difficult question for modern organisations to address and resolve, is that while some organisations and leaders know how crucial 'talent' is for their survival and competitive effectiveness, you can't actually measure and grow anything until you can define exactly what it is, which is the real challenge. I believe that you can only begin to measure and develop anything when you can define exactly what it is. Talent is prime example. The concept of 'talent' alone is completely intangible. It means all sorts of different things to different people and organisations. Therefore, the key to measuring and growing 'talent' is first to define exactly what 'talent' is—to understand and describe what it means, what it looks like, how it behaves and what it can achieve. And these definitions will be different depending on the organisation. Talent in a bank will have a quite different meaning to talent in an advertising agency, or in a hospital. So that's the first answer to the question: First you need to define it and agree the definition, which is likely to be quite an involved and detailed task, because it's such a deep and serious concept...

Aside from defining what talent is, the organisation needs to acknowledge the importance of talent, (according to the agreed organisational definitions). This requires a commitment from the very top, which must be transparent and visible to all. Then people will begin to value talent more fittingly and preciously. A similar thing happened with the 'total quality' concept, when leaders woke up and realized its significance. But they first had to define it and break it down into measurable manageable elements before they could begin to improve it. Talent is the same.

12. Which post would you like to work for?

You can say something commensurate with my knowledge and skills currently, with an opportunity to grow in the job.

13. Why aviation or hospitality industry?

Focus on your people-person skills. Mention you enjoy interacting with people from different walks of life, with diverse castes, cultures and like to bring a smile to their faces, through interaction. You can add you are committed in your carrer choice and currently, it's the most rapidly growing industry.

14. Do you have any job experience?

Mention anything like a summer job at Pizza hut or when you went canvassing for your college. IT training can be mentioned and have the certificate ready with you.

15. What is your commitment to our organisation?

Your answer may be that you are keen to establish yourself, gain hands on experience and are looking at a long-term relationship.

16. Tell us about your family background.

Mention father and mother's job, hierarchy of siblings and their supportive attitude. Also how the atmosphere at home has inspired you towards the current choice.

17. When can you join us?

As soon as possible or as soon as my final exams are complete. But do take the joining letter given out and negotiate this later.

18. What are your salary expectations?

According to company structure and regulations.

19. What training have you got in this line?

Mention any professional course that has helped you to further yourself in this line, giving an outline of topics, subjects covered and also how theory and practical skills were involved.

20. Mention something not in your resume.

You can cover sport achievements, debates or activities you participated in.

21. How does First-Aid training help you in this job?

It has equipped me with knowledge and first-hand experience about how to deal with medical situations common in a flight. I am also aware how to handle medical emergencies, so that passengers' lives or health are not endangered till further aid is possible.

22. What are your strengths?

I am a people's person, flexible, confident, willing to go out of my way open to learning, take orders comfortably, use my intelligence and take decisions as required. I also love to travel and face challenges.

23. What are your weaknesses?

I am an emotional person but I regard this as my strength as I can empathise with a passenger or situation instantly.

24. Why this particular airline interests you? or why this hotel specifically?

It is a reputed organisation, known for its service standards and it will be an honour to be associated with this great brand name and help build it up too. I would love to be a representative ambassador of my country to our valued clients.

25. If a customer is shouting for no valid reason, how will you react?

I will apologise and offer my assistance to rectify the situation immediately.

26. Are you ready to do night shifts?

Yes.

27. Are you ready to travel so far for work daily?

Yes.

28. We have a senior post vacant than the one you are applying for. Would you accept that if it is offered to you?

Yes, I will accept the challenge and do my best with your guidance.

29. If you get a better offer from another place, will you accept it?

I would be grateful for giving me this opportunity. I will prove to be hard working and loyal, making rapid progress and becoming an asset to the organisation.

30. Will you choose a job over a career?

I will opt for a job which is inline with my future in the service industry.

31. What is your job experience?

Mention any jobs you have done, even part time in which capacity and how it has helped you to grow.

32. Why did you quit your previous assignment?

I had to prepare for my graduation exams, which are important for me to enhance myself.

33. What did you learn there?

I learnt how to take decisions, take orders or being in charge. I learnt how to be capable of multi-tasking and taking on additional responsibilities and gained the trust of my seniors.

I also learnt a lot about the industry and honed my skills in computers etc.

34. Why are you looking at an MNC for a job?

I have done my IT training with ....I liked the environment of professionalism and efficiency. I interacted with various types of people and gained experience in handling them and different situations. It has given me more confidence in competing for an assignment here.

35. Describe a memorable moment in your life.

I moved to an independent life, once I started studying in the city and managed alone. It made me mature and confident.

36. Why do you want to be a part of the service industry?

I thrive in a challenging environment. I have a drive to excel in a competitive atmosphere, so a routine 9 to 5 job will stifle me. I also love to interact with people and feel satisfied when there is a smile on their faces.

37. General discussion on ... topic.

Opt to be a team leader, so you can demonstrate your skills as well as knowledge of the topic. Moderate the topic, making all participants open up in a healthy discussion, underline agreements, lead to conclusions and sum it up, allowing consideration for all points of view.

38. How do you take into account the risk factor involved in aviation?

We live in challenging times and events can occur wherever and whenever I am going to be formally trained to deal with medical and serious situations, so I accept this with a positive attitude.

39. Which department are you interested to work in?

I am open to learning all the departments' working. I will, however, be ready to be guided in my choice by my performance after I have been exposed.

40. Why should we select you over other candidates?

I have researched this career line and am committed after having done a training course for a year from... . I firmly believe that my future lies here. I have the requisite skills and attitudes required for this opening have developed my personality accordingly. It is in line with my aptitude and liking for a public dealing job. I enjoy challenges, variety and responsibility, which this job provides.

4l. How long are you looking at working at this job?

I am looking at a long-term career in this field and am willing to invest my productive years here.

42. What other options are you considering if you are not selected here?

I will continue to look for similar opportunities. I am looking at completing my post graduation and have enrolled in a course already. I will keep trying till I succeed. I will prepare myself better for the next opportunity. I may explore retail management and am open to job offers there. However, Aviation is my first love. I will gain experience in related fields and keep applying till I succeed.

43. What would your reaction be if you are finalised today?

Thank you, of course. I will share the good news with my family and friends and celebrate. I will sleep easy tonight, having achieved my life's ambition to work with... . I will celebrate and get set to start my training here.

44. What games do you play? Tell us about it.

I play badminton and participitated at college level tournaments. I play basketball and have represented my state on several occasions. I love cricket and am very involved with the IPL matches, being held currently. I am more of an indoor person, love to read and paint. In school, I enjoyed running and biking though.

45. Are your parents comfortable with this choice?

Yes, they are supportive. They have let me take an independent decision and I would like to prove myself to them. I would like to come upto their expectations and do even better.

46. What influenced your career choice?

I have family/relatives/friends working in this line and am inspired by their experiences. I associate myself with this career option from childhood and want to fulfill my dreams. I have all the skills and personality traits required here and identify with the job. I am influenced by the advertising and would like to be ... personnel positively.

47. What post is acceptable to you?

The job in question is the one I am applying for, according to my qualifications. I would like to start as per company rules and work my way through to seniority. I am open to challenges and willing to take the fast track.

SAMPLE INTERVIEW

- **Good morning, please be seated.**

  Thank you.

- **Please tell us something about yourself.**

  I've just completed a training course for cabin crew from——Institute and am looking forward to a career in Aviation. I am also preparing for graduation in BA Honours in English this year.

- **What attracted you towards this career?**

  (a) I have family and friends who are already in this line and since my early years, I found it very glamorous, visiting different places and earning good money.

  (b) Since my childhood, and through my formative years, it has been a goal I've studied for actively. I am an extrovert and get along with different kinds of people comfortably. I've tested myself by working in a collective environment and handling stalls and people independently. I've enjoyed handling enquiries and have grown at these part-time jobs, through college days. Besides, I love travel and challenges in cultures, food and environment. This has tremendous potential in the current scenario in aviation and I know, I will be an asset to any airline.

- **Why do you prefer this option in service industry?**
  (a) I find flying every attractive and want to see the world.
  (b) It is challenging, and it will make me mature and worldly. It will expose me to international cultures and I would like to be a brand ambassador of the country and airline I represent. I will also be able to pursue higher education through correspondence in my free time. I plan to be in this career for a long time and I am committed to this career line.

- **What do you know about our organisation?**
  (a) I read you website and can give you all the information given.
  (b) It's progressive and at par with international airlines. It has the best growth rate in India and I would like to be associated and to contribute to creating more loyal customers.

- **Where do you see yourself five years from now, if you are selected?**
  (a) I will still be enjoying flying around and will have made many friends around the world.
  (b) I hope to have gained enough experience to move up in the hierarchy and be in a position to contribute, may be in trainings or administration even.

- **Why should we choose you over others, who are here today?**
  (a) I have all the required qualities and will be a dedicated worker.
  (b) I am committed to this career, as I've already been trained for it, with — since 1 year. I've consistently scored well in the personality test and GD's held. I have a natural affinity for a people handling job and held several assignments with corporate collecting data or handling enquiries. The satisfaction is immense for a job well done. I am looking forward to more opportunities.

- **How would you plan your career if you are not shortlisted here?**
  (a) I would prepare myself better and reapply.
  (b) I would take this as a learning experience and build on strengths.

- **Are you ready for a group discussion now?**
  (a) Thank you for the opportunity. Does it mean I have cleared the interview?
  (b) I will aspire to do my best, given the opportunity. Thanks.

The above questions are generally rephrased in various ways: Try to pick the answer most suited to you or plan out your answer according to the guidelines.

★ ★ ★

10. Soft Skills

SOFT SKILLS

These are most desired skills in a service industry job and keep one on the fast track of a chosen career path. Hard skills can be acquired through pursuit of a degree, but soft skills have to be garnered through good education as well as exposure to a conducive home and work environment, which has a relaxing atmosphere, good mentors and competitive edge. Soft skills are most in demand for creating value for the customers be it hospitality, aviation, malls, boutiques, telephone service providers, hospital front desks and restaurants not to mention any consumer durables, MNC's etc.

India is taking fast strides and needs to create a workforce that is competent enough to support India's quality products and services aggressively. Candidates who are technically very skilled cannot migrate into a managerial role and transform to lead a local or a global firm. Technical graduates have a poor rate of employability in the managerial cadre, despite core competence. Service sector desperately needs to benchmark these standards. Soft skills mean greeting with a warm smile, a firm handshake, meticulous time management, impeccable English, effective communication and positive body language. Personal habits and moral values are being ingrained in one's formative years and practised constantly. Most management institutes or finishing and professional courses compulsorily include this in their curriculum.

To develop them in house, activities like serious group discussions, extempore speeches, debates, public speaking, personal interview sessions, presentations on allied topics, news reporting, along with team participation, etc. are covered intensely. Personal grooming and even learning foreign languages add the cutting edge to an unpolished gem. India needs a finished product to put our best forward specially in view of the forthcoming Commonwealth games. We have no dearth of intelligent youth and progressive thinking youngsters. What is needed is some training or guidance in developing one's persona.

SOFT SKILLS CHECKLIST

Having a positive attitude creates a balanced individual who can handle challenges and accept them as an avenue for honing your abilities and showing off your productivity.

Developing leadership qualities and leading others diplomatically is a very critical component most service sector companies need. Communication is an important skill that can lead and guide to a fruitful conclusion. Good body posture, talking logically and persuasively, correct language and listening to others is very essential.

Being confident, and building on one's strengths, innovative thinking are facets of a balanced personality, taking negative feedback from your superiors in a positive way, as well as also being sensitive to others' perceptions handling it constructively are also musts.

Leading by example is most effective in motivating and innovative task-handling situations. In order to be effective in your work place, one needs to delegate tasks, manage different activities and also report to superiors. Risk-taking is an essential element of maturity, necessary when handling ever-charging dynamics of interaction with different people and situations daily.

Soft skills can be acquired with practice, *i.e.*, IT, practical and mechanical skills, problem-solving, personality development, written and verbal ability, etc. Time management is another critical skill to be an effective employee. "Plan, schedule and prioritize" are the keywords for productivity.

Set up time for having meeting, talking individually to clients. Genius do not let visitors and idle phone calls steal their precious resource. If the customer needs something to be done urgently, try to accommodate in the company's best interests. Be disciplined and communicate respect in your tone.

★ ★ ★

11. Group Discussions & Group Dynamics

GROUP DISCUSSIONS

It is done to identify team players and those with leadership qualities. A topic is given to each team and participation is evaluated, within a given time span. Topics can be general like "global warning and its effects" or "should a career be individual or a family one". Your presentation skills, etiquettes, fair play, your awareness of the topic–all indicate your understanding of the topic. There is a summing up finally. One should be assertive enough to put forward one's viewpoint across convincingly without being dominating.

Being a good listener is as critical as being a good capable orator. Add on a new point or lead to a positive conclusion.

Prepare for a GD, read newspapers, listen to news, surf the net for information, interact with people from diverse backgrounds, networking or most important, desire to be aware of the world around you, will have the desired effect. If asked to lead, initiate the topic interestingly and then throw it open for discussion. Sum it up periodically and lead to a positive conclusion.

Some critical points are to be practised. Everyone contributes all viewpoints and observes key points scored. Speaking for too long or too loudly, too much or cutting another, getting personal or abusive is considered negatively. In a personal interview, the focus is on you as a person, your goals, attitude, interests, strengths and weaknesses. Analyze your goals and how to achieve what you want. Be honest, yet realistic. Your responses under pressure will indicate your ability to handle the situation, in a positive manner. Dress in formal attire as per code as indicated. Be punctual, confident and present your resume, certificates and photos when asked. Provide your contact numbers and email on your CV. Always part positively, with a smile.

GROUP DYNAMICS

Candidates will be subject to group dynamics test, where their ability to work together will be tested. Candidates must understand the concept, so they may participate with confidence and give intelligent responses to the candidates.

A group is a collection of people. Creating awareness of their own membership and goals, they define the problem solving process to achieve them. As humans, we are social animals and have an interest in society. We are born into a family, we get educated and work in groups, we play and worship in groups. Even one's identity is formed with our interaction with others and most of our goals can be achieved only with the co-operation and co-ordination of others. Pooling of resources to accomplish common objectives, results in advantages for each member that he or she could never enjoy through individual action. Our psychological health too depends on managing our relationships with others effectively. The group in turn creates the individual's formation of attitude and tends to develop response patterns to situations. An individual's habits, attitudes, skills, aspirations and shaping the perception of his own self in a role or given situation, expressing themselves positively or negatively and making choices, with accuracy and speed—all this is determined by group dynamics.

Groups develop a number of dynamic processes that separate them from a random collection of individuals. These include norms, roles, relations, need to belong, social influence and effects on behaviour.

Team Building

Individuals working in groups are observed as per the following norms:

1. How they work more effectively in groups;
2. The benefits they reap of a collective decision;
3. How they communicate with other group members;
4. How they increase the cohesiveness of the group;
5. How they analyze advantages and disadvantages of diversity;
6. How new members get socialized with the group;
7. How new effective norms are developed.

Above points are very important known to make your response impressive on the GD.

Advantages of Group Dynamics

Each member learns:

1. How to recognize and overcome personal weaknesses?
2. How to acknowledge and build other's thoughts?
3. How to help another to develop synergy within the group?

Instead of competition, class members become comrades, building mutual respect to maintain networking, maintaining relationships throughout their professional life.

Developing Group Dynamics

1. The voice of each individual counts, so listen;
2. Participate and encourage all to contribute;
3. Build the story being candid with as well as respectful of others;
4. Take responsibility for your actions and reactions;
5. Remember forcing on weaknesses undermines, but focusing on strengths supports;
6. Know you weaknesses so you can grow, know your strengths so you can stretch;
7. Standby your convictions, but remember the group is not always right or wrong, and neither are you;
8. Realities must be attended to;
9. Characteristics of interplay, honesty and fairness will emerge clearly, during interaction;
10. Understand what's in the box, so you can think outside of it.

12. Important Components of Training Given to Cabin Crew

STUDY MATERIAL

Once recruited as a crew member, you complete a mandatory 2/3 months training course, which is governed by the Civil Aviation Authority. It includes a safety and emergency procedures module, paid for by the airline. The instructors are airline employees and experienced senior crew members. A stipend is paid during the training period. Students are trained on:

Air craft orientation, ditching, decompression, fire fighting, passenger management, security-related issues, extraordinary issues, first aid and survival techniques. Some of the training is conducted with different simulators to perform the drill and procedures needed to deal with different types of emergencies for safety. Language labs, fire and smoke mock-ups, ditching practice equipment are all part of the extensive trainings. All this is really expensive so the airlines may take a security deposit from the candidates to ensure that they are under contract for a minimum period of 2-3 years. The fee is refunded to the candidate if he continues to work beyond the minimum number of years.

Once the training is completed, tests are administered and ranking is given. Now, they get their "wings" literally! Probation may vary from 3-6 months, after which their performance is assessed by the check crew members in-flight. Lastly, candidates are confirmed as permanent or contractual employees and salary benefits start accruing.

An assessment is done after an interval of 12 months, as well as retesting, to ensure quality of service and knowledge. A recurrent training is also done, along with testing, to ensure quality standards and knowledge levels.

SUBSEQUENT INFORMATION USEFUL TO CABIN CREW

1. **Stopover Health Advice-** How to adapt to different climates and keep healthy, with a variety of food/cultures etc?
2. **Phoning Home-** How to use public phone, list of ISD codes to be dialed from different locations, "calling from a mobile" familiarisation?

3. **World Guides-** Featuring all destinations, including tips on culture and lifestyle of other countries and emergency contact details.

4. **How to Dress and Code of Conduct-** Giving vital information on climate, etiquettes and guides and hierarchy of reporting on stopovers.

Training Topics

Emergency procedures	Civil aviation authorities
Passenger handling	Dangerous goods and security
Security procedures	Emergency equipments
Fire fighting	First-aid techniques
In-flight procedures	Aviation terminology
Human factors	Turbulence
Ditching	Crowd control and pilot incapacitation
Survival	Self-defense technique
Safety procedures	Psychology
The organisation of flight and communications	Tasks and responsibilities
Operating door exits Hygiene/ food handling service/galley/ ethics/good manners/ on board sales training, etc.	Crew resource management

IN-FLIGHT ENTERTAINMENT (IFE)

It refers to entertainment available to passengers during a flight. After World War II, it was basically food and drink services, along with an occasional projector movie during lengthy flights, on a screen at the front of the cabin, which could be heard via a headphone socket at his/her seat. Today, IFE is offered on board in all wide-body aircraft. Narrow bodied jets are limited due to space, storage and weight limits. Some airlines are on demand though.

The system affects safety of the aircraft, so it is made independent of the main power source and processor. Airlines capitalize on providing state-of-art entertainment and may charge a user fee based on individual use or tend to get a majority of the cost paid for by advertisement on IFE.

Varieties Offered

- ***Audio Entertainment:*** It includes music, news, information and shows, not to mention latest movies. Most channels are prerecorded, have a variety of news, information, movies, music, popular shows. Some airlines provide a channel devoted to the plane's radio communication, allowing passengers to listen in on the pilot's conversation with the other pilot and ground stations. This is provided via headphones, plugged into seat pockets and with a channel selector and volume control switch located in the armrest of the seat.

- ***Personal Televisions:*** They are located in seat backs and show direct broadcast live television as well as video games. On demand systems enable passengers to forward, pause and rewind at will as well as select individual programmes to see.
- ***Moving Map System or Air Show:*** It is real time flight information. It displays a map, showing direction and position of the plane, also giving air specs, distance to destination, altitude, local time, etc.
- ***Wi-Fi:*** Internet is provided through a satellite network through air-to-ground network. Passengers can connect via their laptops.
- ***Mobile Phone Connectivity:*** Airlines are testing sending and receiving messages, but not making or receiving calls on board their flights. Possibly if it is successful, it may provide voice calls and usage of mobile phones on board.

DUTY FREE SALES SERVICE

This is sale of liquor/cigarettes, luxury items like branded watches, sunglasses, jewelry, perfumes etc. on board to international passengers. The price list and brochure are provided and payment can be made by cash or by card in the acceptable international currencies. The cabin crew has to conduct this service post meal and enjoy a commission on sales concluded. A record of sales and money collected is to be submitted at the destination, as well as a take-over done at originating station.

MEAL SERVICES

This is often a USP of airlines who pride themselves for good variety, exotic choice in beverages and meals, as well as the quality of service this is dispensed with. Often passengers select airlines to fly, based on their services. The ambience is as critical to the entire experience as much as the spread of items. The beverage variety includes soft drinks, beers, wines, champagnes to cocktails and liqueurs. The art of serving is finely honed during training and nuances of fine dining experience have to be inculcated along with knowledge of wines and food.

Service in the first class requires special knowledge and expertise and cabin crew have to be specially groomed for this. It's a very critical component of the entire in flight experience and majorly contributes to a memorable flying experience, hence its importance for cabin crew.

The passenger wants to use his travelling time to the maximum. Enjoying a tasty meal is the perfect way to arrive at one's destination energized and ready for leisure or business. It also contributes to a well-looked after feeling.

The flight crew need catering that is easy to handle and is utmost space saving, whilst being a pleasure to serve. Dispatchers and handlers need a fast and simple ordering system. Caterers provide a wide selection of international and local dishes, eye-catching snacks and meals presented in attractive and disposable packaging. Healthy and balanced meals in a stylish environment and served with care, is an experience to die for. At affordable prices, these delicacies are prepared by a team of professionals with many years of experience in the hospitality industry. The packaging has to be space saving and tamper proof too. The food is generally hygienically sealed and packed in convenient cooled cases, so there is no spoilage and spillage. The number of items, quality and quantity may fluctuate due to shifts in economies of the airline industry.

The prominent caterers in India are Ambassador Hotel, Oberoi Flight Services and Tajsats. They cater to domestic airlines like Jetlite and Air India, as well as international airlines like Lufthansa, Swissair, Saudia etc. The catering units work 24x7, offering regional authentic cuisines, as well as Chinese, Continental and Italian or any specific request of a client of airline. Whenever the President/Prime Minister is travelling on overseas trips, these units are engaged to provide the required expertise.

Most airlines on international sectors provide an excellent choice in meals and beverages. A variety of cuisines are offered. It is the USP of most airlines and a definite pull to lure worldly passengers. An in-flight meal is served at 30,000 ft while being prepared sometimes much in advance at a catering unit, dedicated to flight services. The first flight kitchen was set up in 1936 for United Airlines, in USA.

More and more airlines are now employing renowned chefs to plan their menu and also educate catering and airline employees how to prepare and serve a meal conceptualized by them. These meals vary widely in quality and quantity across different classes and airlines, from a simple beverage in a short-haul flight to a 7 course gourmet meal. Preserving freshness is a particular challenge, as is catering to travellers of different ages, ethnicity, and taste options. Menus are created to cater to the time of the day and duration of the flight.

Short-haul Meal—It can be served as "one tray" or for first class; it can be a table layout with metal cutlery and glassware. Special meals like baby meals, medical meals, low or high fibre diet, low salt/low calorie, bland, etc. even diabetic are all arranged with prior notice. Even religious needs are met with i.e. Kosher or Muslim meal. Children's meals can contain items enjoyed by them like chips, soft drinks, chocolates, baked beans, sandwiches, hot dogs and hamburgers.

Long Haul Flights—In business or first class, most European and American airlines serve multi course gourmet meals. Delicacies like caviar, fine champagne and choice of accompanying wines is available. Financial pressures have currently restricted airlines to budget their meals or serve small snacks. The low cost ones may offer only bottled water or sell prepacked boxes at a price. Taste is still of consideration though and every effort is made to maintain freshness and supply universal appeal items.

Technical crew meals are strictly-monitored, avoiding egg and dietary products. The position of the crew member determines his meal output. No two operating crew are served the same items, to ensure minimizing risk of pilots on board being ill.

Cutlery—Now due to security threat, standard stainless steel has been replaced with plastic ones, at least in economy class. Items like knives and forks were evaluated closely for their potential use as a weapon on the aircraft. The non-food items like salt/pepper and sugar are supplied in sachets. A moist towellette is provided in the meal tray, along with salad dressing, toothpicks and after mint.

Will in flight food service of the future more closely resemble restaurant-quality dining? Unfortunately, the value passengers place on meals in selecting airlines is difficult to quantify, so airlines have very little hard data to motivate them. However, new food preparation technology and the continuing grumble of passengers' stomachs will hopefully move airlines to continue to improve food quality in the air.

Choice of Meals—To ensure your choice of meal on board, you need to inform the airline about your special meal preference while booking the ticket. Ask your travel agent to enter the appropriate meal code. To ensure that you get the best possible service, ask the reservation staff for the special meals available at the time of reserving your seat. Please make your special meal request at least 24 hours prior to flight departure. For bookings made within 24 hours, vegetarian meals will be provided.

Ensure that your travel agent carries forward the special meal requests when bookings are amended (i.e. change of itinerary / reinstatement / change in class of travel etc.) If not, the special meal request will not be catered for, even if the request was inserted in the initial booking, and a vegetarian meal will then be served.

All special meals like diabetic meal (DBML), low cholesterol (LFML), low sodium (LSML), low calorie (LCML), low protein (LPML), non lactose meal (NLML) and no salt (NSML) have vegetarian or non-vegetarian options. Please ensure that your agent always prefixes an SPML (Special Meal) for NVML (Non Vegetarian) and JNML (Jain Meal).

CATEGORIES OF MEALS

The meal services are divided into major and minor. Major consists of breakfast, lunch and dinner and minor is generally snacks and beverages.

***Breakfast*—**It could be continental, consisting of juice, tea/coffee, preserves with croissant. American has a hot meal component in addition to comprising eggs, potatoes in some form and maybe sausages or ham. Often, yoghurt is served to enable digestion. The type of breakfast served depends on the interval between meal times. Joining passengers could be offered continental when it is late for an American breakfast.

Lunch/Dinner—This consists of a main entree, vegetarian or non-veg, comprising a vegetable, some variety of pulao and a chicken or fish gravy dish. In case of veg, it is a veg curry generally. There is a salad with dressing, dessert, bread roll along with tea/coffee and chocolates. In first class, it is mostly five courses, consisting of soup and appetizers, salad, main entree, dessert, topped off with cheese and fruits. Last but not the least, passengers enjoy a choice of liqueurs or tea/ coffee at the end. It may be a full restaurant type experience to a faster express meal in the business class or simply a snack, if you are feeling peckish. In Y class, it is a standard meal made of the best choice in items that the country can offer. In India, the choice is very vast due to regional cuisines.

Supper—can be served for joining passengers. It is given when there are late night joinees on board from a transit point. It is a light meal, maybe more snacky than a proper meal and just enough to hold passengers till the next service.

Snack Service—is a light meal, served at tea time, along with tea /coffee. There is a confectionary and a savoury item, brownie or sandwiches, along with sauce etc. It is prepacked boxes, sold at a cost in low cost carriers, but served warmly in case of other classes of travel. Tea/coffee or soft drinks are also given to accompany. In non-veg, the items may be chicken tikka, seekh kebab in addition to cutlets or patties. A combination of factors determines contents like time between meals and duration of the flight. If interval between two meal times is not much, a light snack is provided or only joining passengers are given a snack.

Beverage Service—may be a welcome drink like lime juice or individually packed juice in cartons, served after boarding is complete. On the other hand, it may be an alcoholic service conducted prior to a main meal. Generally, two rounds of a 30 ml serving are given per passenger, along with a savoury in Y class. In first class, you could enjoy whisky, Bacardi, rum and coke, vodka or wines and even champagne. Cocktails and mocktails are made for each passenger, at his request and served with endless variety of small eats as accompaniments. The spread has visual appeal and taste unlimited!

Note: There are various points to be kept in mind while serving meals. As every airline invests in dieticians to give them balanced, healthy meals, suitable to passengers of all ages, nationalities, it is critical that meals are conducted in a manner most conducive to enhancing the experience. Meals should be heated to its ideal temperature, and as close to serving time, so that they are edible and presentable. Make sure the meals are thawed out. Along with this, training is also imparted about the method of service to be used. In the first/executive class, it is a 5 course meal service accompanied with a select range of wines and hard liquor, only on international flights of course.The most expensive items are on the menu, choice of entrees is plenty and infinite variety panders to all tastes. All dinnerware is the finest brand in chinaware and cutlery is stainless steel. In Y class, it is mostly plastic ware in a single serve tray, with limited choice and in set quantities. Only soft drinks and at the most, two complimentary alcoholic drinks per person are allowed.

MEAL SHORTAGE

Just as airlines bet on no-shows in over-selling a flight, they also bet on no-shows when estimating the number of meals needed. As a result, meal shortages are not uncommon. Industry-wide, it is estimated that meal shortages run about 0.8% per day, though this has been reduced from 1.2% in 1998.

According to a recent article in USA Today, most domestic airlines are increasing their food service expenditures, including meal counts. (However, many cut back in the 90s, so an increase may just mean getting back to what we've come to expect.) All in all, potential meal shortages are just one more reason to sit up front.

SAMPLE MENUS FOR EACH SERVICE, ON INTERNATIONAL ROUTES

Breakfast—Breakfast is available on flights departing before 10 a.m. An assortment of gourmet cheese and crackers, accompanied by a fresh seasonal fruit mixture, fresh yogurt and one of the following: Banana mini-loaf; Raspberry breakfast cake; Danish pastry.

Lunch and Dinner—Served on flights departing from 10 a.m. to 8 p.m. All salads are accompanied by a selection of fresh, seasonal mixed fruit.

Turkey and Bacon Cobb Salad: Crisp romaine lettuce topped with diced roasted turkey, chopped bacon, diced tomatoes, sliced black olives, diced Swiss cheese, and hardboiled egg wedges served with a balsamic vinaigrette dressing. Served with a selection of fresh fruit.

Julienne Chef Salad: Crisp romaine lettuce topped with Black Forest ham, julienne oven roasted turkey breast, Napa cabbage, shredded cheddar cheese, diced tomato, chopped black olives, and sliced hardboiled egg served with a ranch dressing. Served with a selection of fresh fruit.

Grilled Asian Chicken Salad: Grilled Asian chicken breast served with a blend of radicchio and Napa cabbage along with fresh cilantro, cucumbers, and julienne carrots, served with an Asian Sesame ginger dressing. Served with a selection of fresh fruit.

Sandwich Wraps—Served on flights departing from 10 a.m. to 8 p.m. Each wrap is served with a bag of chips.

Smoked Turkey and Swiss Club Wrap: Thinly-sliced mesquite turkey breast and turkey bacon, topped with crisp romaine lettuce, cucumber, tomato, red onion, and Swiss cheese, with a spinach cream cheese spread on a flour tortilla.

Grilled Tuscan Chicken, Salami Wrap: Sliced marinated chicken breast, thinly-sliced Genoa salami and Provolone cheese, topped with baby spinach, shredded Napa cabbage, roasted red tomato and kalamata olives, with a basil garlic cream cheese spread on a flour tortilla.

Turkey, Cheddar and Asparagus Wrap—Sliced oven roasted turkey breast and cheddar cheese, topped with shredded Napa cabbage, baby spinach, asparagus and roasted red tomato, with a spinach cream cheese spread on a flour tortilla.

SAFETY EQUIPMENT ʼAMILIARIZATION

This is mandatory, prescribed by DGCA, as the primary reason why crew were required on board a commercial flight. It was to ensure their safety during a flight.

Crews are familiarized with all the locations, operations and use of equipment provided aboard. Hands-on exposures are provided in depth on simulators, which are actual models of aircraft. Equipment handling is compulsory. The crew need to know where to locate the prescribed equipment, how many pieces are available on that particular model of air craft and how to put it to use effectively.

The cabin crew need to be familiar with the safety demonstration also, so they can follow prescribed procedures prior to take-off, on every flight. They also have to learn how to operate doors prior take-off, landing and how to arm/disarm them at destinations or ground halts.

They have to operate the safety evacuation slides and know the fine drill procedures, ditching, basic communication norms on board and also get familiarized with pilot incapacitation if it happens during a scheduled flight. They may have to even land a plane, with ground assistance through wireless communication, in such an event.

Thus, this is a very critical component of cabin crew training and the skills can mean a difference between life and death, in an emergency situation. The cabin crew are the saviours of the passengers and it is their presence of mind that saves lives and ensures minimal damage to the aircraft.

Even in hijacking or terrorist activities, related techniques are imparted, so that cabin crew can deter any disastrous consequences. This truly determines the calibre of a responsible organisation, committed to "quality service before self".

FIRST-AID TRAINING

(a) Medical Situations

Use caution and act according to company proceedings, passenger situation and do not discuss with others. Give personal medication. Check if it is prescribed for his condition. Inform the captain to determine hospitalization or ambulance. Ask for a doctor on board, if situation is serious enough. Serious burns, fractures, bleeding, etc. must be attended to immediately. The cabin report must include information and be countersigned by the captain.

Effects of Flight on Body: The gas filled cavities in the body need to be balanced with atmospheric pressure. Effects are enhanced on landing, i.e., cold can cause severe ear bleeding. Use nose drops, pinch nose tip. Swallow or breathe deeply. Kids should be fed.

Sinus cavities are linked to the nose by narrow tunnels and can even result in nose bleed, when severe. Deep seated fillings in teeth or declaration of degeneration of muscles can cause severe toothache.

Having carbonated drinks, cabbage and onions can also cause additional discomfort.

In first aid, accident victims get help. Inform captain and obtain site medical assistance by radio, if required. Start life saving aid. Give O_2 supply and ensure circulation. Initiate ordinary first aid. Keep the body warm, cover wounds, relieve pain, immobilize fractures, make the passenger comfortable and give relief by keeping them informed. Don't panic or display that the situation is not under control. Ask for any medicines if available with passenger or if he has a previous history.

The Aero-medical course for cabin crew is mandatory and prescribed by DGCA. A certificate is awarded at its completion. It is normally sourced out to Red Cross or well-known hospices use Apollo. A recurrent training is also given after intervals to all cabin crew. It is an interactive classroom course in medical treatment led by an instructor. It can be customized for each airline, physically practised on board; a demonstration is prepared for practical lessons in the classroom. The main objective is to familiarize cabin crew also with the human body and symptoms of the medical condition that might occur on board. It will enable you to make the decision about what the passenger is suffering from and what course of treatment to follow. It is divided into ten sections:

1. Skeletal and muscular system.
2. Nervous system.
3. Cardio-vascular.
4. Respiratory and immune system.
5. Digestive and urinary system.
6. General knowledge and first aid.
7. Breathing and heart problems.
8. Bleeding, fractures and concussions.
9. Epilepsy,diabetes and asthma
10. Childbirth, abdominal disorders, burns and malaria.

Medical Equipment on Board

Different airlines carry different equipment. The contents often depend on travel time and destination. Doctor's kit is generally put on board if flying time is 90 minutes over water. First-Aid kit is made up of bandboxes, disposable gloves, burn and wound dressing, safety pins, scissors, tapes, antiseptic cleaner, analgesic, adhesive tape, disposable resuscitation aid, nasal decongestant, antacid and anti-diarrhoea. A handbook of basic information is also kept in the box, with a complete list of medicines and information of side effects of medicines in at least English and one other language.

Emergency Equipment

This is to be used only by doctors or nurses on board, if any. Additional medicine and equipment include saline solution, syringes, needles, digene, anti-spasm, blood pressure measuring device, sphysmanometer, pharyngeal airway tubes and angina pectoris medicines.

BASIC MEDICAL KNOWLEDGE

This is very strictly adhered to, as it is a critical component in being an accomplished cabin crew, capable of rendering required emergency aid, during a flight.

The main topics covered are as below:

1. **Angina pectoris:** In Latin, it means chest pain. There is pain behind the chest plate patient is pale, has nausea and breaks into cold sweat. It is caused by the calcification of coronary arteries, giving blood and O_2. Narrow arteries provide less O_2, leading to a painful sensation in the chest. Stress is also a factor.

   Treatment: Make the patient comfortable, loosening clothing and ensuring rest. Give medicine available on board, based on company regulations. Stay with the passenger, give psychological support. A landing may be necessary, if decided on by the captain.

2. **Shock:** It is life-threatening and occurs when blood flow is reduced. Normally, it worsens and immediate aid is needed. It is a leading cause of death. Patient is cold and sweating, has vomiting, breathes fast, pulse is rapid from 120-140, compared to normal 60/beats per min.

   Treatment: Place in a comfortable warm position, raising lower limbs. Check for injuries. Support with pillows below legs. Oxygen may be given but no fluids. Wet lips if patient insists. Give psychological aid. Make sure he wears warm but light clothing, making sure air passage is free. Do not move, if there is an injury. Give CPR if necessary.

3. **Bleeding:** Normal adult has 5 litres of blood in his body or 70 ml per kg of ideal wt. A loss of up to 15% of total volume can be endured. Bleeding can be arterial or Venal.

   External Bleeding: Blood comes out in tight red spurts, circulation is less, so bleeding is difficult to stop, and must be pressed directly. An air sickness bag can then be placed over nose and mouth. Raise injured part. Check breathing and for shock immediately.

   Internal Bleeding: Steady flow of maroon blood coagulation is caused and it is easier to control. Prevent shock by direct pressure. Raise injured part, if there is no bleeding from the heart. Put bandage, do not move.

   Heavy internal bleeding can occur near broken bones or near an injured area by an accident. It can be untraced and is generally painful. Patient can be unconscious or drowsiness is apparent. Blood may be passed from rectum, ears and nose or due to miscarriage. External bleeding comes from low blood pressure and fainting can occur. It may not be possible to stop the blood flow, so captain may decide on an unscheduled landing.

4. **Dislocation:** The auricular head glides out of the synovial capsule. There is swelling, tenderness, sharp pain and inability to move. Prevent shock. Do not attempt to replace the dislocation, but take professional help, if available.

5. **Wounds:** These are generally not sterile, unless in a medical environment. Rinsing with water and soap and bandaging it is possible. Deep gaping wounds should not be tampered with if assistance is available. Otherwise do as above and observe.

Punctured wounds or dust/dirt in them need to be prevented from infection, *i.e.*, with a tetanus injection. Sores also should be treated similarly.

6. **Breathing:** A continuous supply of oxygen is required by various organs to function normally. When there is no fresh supply, cardiac arrest occurs in 3 or 4 minutes and the person is brain dead after 10 minutes. Lack of oxygen in body tissues is called "Hypoxia". It can occur if there is reduction of O_2 content in the air, pneumonia or an obstruction of air way by injuring infectionless haemoglobin. If Hypoxia is not recognized, it is fatal. Symptoms can be blue lips and noise, impaired judgement, dizziness. Decompression in a flight occurs due to a decrease in cabin pressure. There are fixed O_2 masks which fall automatically to provide relief to passengers.
7. **Stroke:** A serious accident, bleeding, lack of O_2 or arterial rupture can lead to this. *Symptoms:* Numbness as sensory sensations are reduced, loss or altered vision, slurred speech, total loss of memory, loss of balance and headache, part paralysis of face. *Treatment:* Maintain blood circulation and breathing by administering or keep the patient warm and comfortable. Generally, captain will opt for an unscheduled landing.
8. **Fracture:** It is a break in the bone by direct or indirect force. Bruising, tenderness, swelling or shortening of the limb with abnormal sensations are predominant symptoms. It is best to get professional help. Use splints to immobilise above and below the fracture.
9. **Head Trauma:** A serious wound, which is visible, results in a typical loss of sight, blurred vision, vomiting, with blood fluids oozing out. Stabilize head and neck and give sterile pressure, check pulse and give O_2, without moving the passenger. Get professional help immediately.
10. **Sprain:** It is a ligament injury in a joint. There is tenderness and pain. Reduce pressure. Swelling is obvious. Use an elastic bandage and do not move the patient.
11. **Choking:** When the airway is blocked or if food is in trachea instead of the esophagus. Brain damage or asphyxia is common. Do not leave the patient alone till the foreign body is out. Patient gasps, cannot talk and has a bluish face colour. It is a life-threatening situation. A cardiac arrest will occur.

    Treatment: Put pressure in the abdomen; with hand between shoulder blades, compress abdomen by putting pressure above navel. Push fist inwards to increase pressure in the chest to push out the obstruction. If patient is unconscious, open mouth and inspect air ways. Perform ventilation and repeat till object comes out loose or help arrives.
12. **Hyper Ventilation:** When a person breathes faster than necessary, the CO_2 level is low. Heaviness of the chest, with pain and headache occur. Stress and anxiety and shock can cause it to happen.

Treatment: Restore balance of O_2 and CO_2 levels by limiting inhalations. Talk or breathe into a paper box covering nose and mouth, while sitting in a comfortable position. If there is no paper box available, breathe into closed fist or even hand and mouth. Give psychological aid.

Unconsciousness: When a patient does not respond to any stimuli externally or due to dehydration or low blood sugar, mental status changes. It is a medical emergency. Check blood circulation, breathing and airways. Begin CPR. Raise feet to get blood to the brain. No food or drink to be given in this state.

13. **Air Sickness:** Aircraft movement or difference in atmospheric pressures can cause motion sickness in normal and healthy people. The inner ear registers motion charges. Symptoms are nausea, clamminess, and loss of appetite, skin pales, and cold sweat. Passenger can also be incapacitated.

    If a passenger is fatigued and anxious, it can affect him more as well as if he is under influence of drugs and alcohol.

    Treatment: Make the passenger comfortable, give first aid and medication. A cool handkerchief on the forehead can lessen the symptoms.

    'Y' Class Syndrome: This is risk of a deep vein thrombosis when travelling long distance by air. Pulmonary embolism and dehydration happens. Prevention is drinking plenty of fluids, not coffee or alcohol though. Calf muscle exercises, rotating ankles and lifting thighs, massaging calves or simply walking after intervals will relieve cramps.

EXERCISES FOR SELF-ASSESSMENT

1. In situations where no O_2 is being inhaled, unconsciousness will occur after 2 minutes, Irreversible brain damage after 4 min, and brain death after 5 minutes.
2. When there is complete obstruction and the patient is unconscious, perform push and pump and repeat until the object comes loose.
3. If someone is choking never give anything to eat or drink.
4. A paper bag can be used when dealing with hyper-ventilation as board.
5. In case of choking, make the person cough it out.
6. To deliver O_2 is the most common way to treat a person who has just woken up after fainting.
7. A passenger who is breathing rapidly has a headache and numbness in hands and lips, should be asked to breathe slowly.
8. A passenger who has blue hands/nails and a terrible headache, administer coffee.
9. A passenger who has fainted, but still has a normal pulse, put in recovery position and administer O_2.
10. A passenger, who is having difficulty in breathing, should loosen his clothing and sit in recovery position.

11. Fist aid kit should include (bandages, syringes, atropine, dioxin, catheter, First-aid hand book, and so on.
12. State correct priority order when starting first-aid:

    Get help, serve coffee, cover wounds, start giving first-aid, give psychological aid, relieve pain, prevent shock, prevent the accident by adequate breathing, immobilize fracture, open airway, sufficient circulation, prevent shock.
13. If a patient is worried about risks of deep vein thrombosis, make the passenger move and rotate his feet.
14. Passenger has a terrible headache due to partying before the flight. Serve him coffee / hot buns.
15. A passenger has been repeatedly to the toilet and is complaining of loose motions. (Give antidiarrhoea medicine from the first-aid kit).
16. A passenger faints but is breathing and has a normal pulse (put him in an appropriate position).
17. A passenger complains about nausea, vomiting and fatigue (tell him to swallow and yawn deeply).
18. A passenger has terrible pain in his ears during descent (give analgesic from first-aid kit).
19. The sinuses are cavities located above the nose within the bones of face and skull.
20. The inner *ear* balances and registers motion charges.

AGGRESSIVE AND INCITING BEHAVIOUR FROM PASSENGERS

This also compromises the safety of other passengers, crew and aircraft. So cabin crew is taught how to handle such situations from soft handling to restraint. Crew must be firm and authoritative in handling disruptive passengers or troublemakers. They can always ask the senior crew or supervisor to handle the situation, if needed. Last but not least, the captain needs to be informed too.

Cabin Crew Training Is Codified

For the first time ever, training of aircraft cabin crew has been brought under regulations issued officially by the DGCA on March 2010, wherein those aspiring to be cabin crew will need to be trained in various aspects that include handling of passengers "who are intoxicated with alcohol or are under the influence of drugs or are aggressive".

SECURITY MEASURES FOR AIRLINES

Cabin crews are involved in this activity when passengers are on board. They have to be vigilant and observant as to what is going on during the flight as well as when the aircraft is on ground, in between flights or turnaround sectors. All passengers' goods must be taken care of, though it is announced on transits, to carry their hand baggage with them. Any suspicious activity by crew or service personnel must be guarded against. When passengers embark with some bulky or unwieldy items, they may be given to the crew to store on board. The baggage must be tagged and stamped by security and handed back to the passenger before he disembarks. Keeping track of passengers during a flight is also a critical situation *i.e.*, if a passenger is fidgeting or making suspicious movements or going to the toilets repeatedly. Monitor for smoking, and be careful to identify any dangerous goods, if carried by any passenger unwittingly. Crew are familiarized with all the categories and UN markings and should know how to deal with them, after taking them from the passenger and informing supervisor and captain. A logbook record is also maintained for any untoward incident.

After passengers disembark at the final stop, take a quick walk around cabin to assess that no glasses, documents or belongings are left behind. They can be handed over to ground staff, to return to passengers in the arrivals lounge. All aircraft are parked in well-lit bays and designated areas. They should keep a distance from surrounding enclosures or other easily forced barriers. Aircraft are generally left under strict surveillance and no unauthorized person gets access to them doing ground halts. No smoking is strictly to be followed and movement of security, ground staff, and maintenance personnel is also to be scrutinised.

Runaway conditions are maintained by technicians on ground and refueling is done under supervision. Glycol urea and acetate are used in ice conditions, as they are quick-acting, have low freezing point and very little environmental impact. The airport authorities are responsible for safe flying and take-off conditions.

SELF-TEST FOR SAFETY MEASURES

1. The passenger's having to undergo a **security** check for their baggage as well as **frisking** personally.
2. Liquids are not carried unless packed **separately** in a pouch for special screening.
3. Passenger cannot carry any **matches and lighters** as part of their hand baggage.
4. A safety drill is demonstrated **prior** to take off.
5. A **safety instruction card** is compulsory in every seat packet in an aircraft.
6. The **oxygen masks** drop down, automatically in decompression during a flight.
7. The **over wing** exit doors can be used in emergency situations additionally.
8. There are **life rafts** available on board.
9. The emergency landing can mean a **slide** operation.
10. There is always a **fire service** at airports.
11. The **fire extinguishers** are red in colour.
12. There are **asbestos gloves** in cockpit for a fire situation.
13. The toilets have an emergency **call bell,** incase needed.
14. The aircraft equipped with a **first-aid** kit.
15. There are **smoke** detectors in the cabin.
16. The **exit** signs are always lit up in a flight.
17. The captain speaks to the ATC through **wireless** technology.
18. There are announcements made for a **doctor** incase of a medical emergency.
19. Provision can be made for a passenger to travel on a **stretcher** with prior intimation.
20. The cabin crew **disarm** doors after touchdown.

TIME DIFFERENCE TRAINING: THE 24-HOUR CLOCK

Most airlines use the 24-hour clock system when telling time. They use this system when assigning trip departures, check-in times and other forms of time designation. The 24-hour clock alleviates communication problems and is more convenient.

Typically, people tell time using a 12-hour clock (the numbers 1 through 12), and adding "a.m." or "p.m." to indicate morning or afternoon. Using the 24-hour clock system, you count each hour from 0 to 23 (because there are 24 hours in a day). When you reach 12 o'clock noon, you continue to count from 12 to 13 (13:00 is 1:00 p.m., 14:00 is 2:00 p.m., 15:00 is 3:00 p.m., etc.) around the clock, until you reach 23:00 or midnight.

At 24:00, you start again from the beginning-00:00 (which is also considered midnight) to 00:01 (one minute after midnight) to 00:02, 00:03, 00:04...0:05, 01:00 (which is 1:00 a.m.), 01:01,01:02, 01:03, 01:59, 02:00, etc.

The following breaks down "a.m." and "p.m." hours.

00:01 to 11:59 = a.m. hours   12:00 = noon

12:01 to 23:59 = p.m. hours   24:00/00:00 = midnight

When reading the 24-hour clock: 10:00 is "ten hundred," 05:40 is "five forty," 00:30 is "zero thirty" and 19:45 is "nineteen forty-five."

When using the 24-hour clock system, it is not necessary to place colons between hours and minutes, or use the a.m. or p.m. designators. For example:

12-Hour Clock	24-Hour Clock
3:00 a.m.	0300
3:00 p.m.	1500
6:15 p.m.	1815
12:01 a.m.	0001

US/Canada Time Zones

The United States and Canada lie within eight standard time zones. Each of these zones uses a time one hour different from its neighboring zone. The hours are earlier to the west of each zone and later to the east.

The following is a list of time zones:

AST	Atlantic Standard Time	PST	Pacific Standard Time
EST	Eastern Standard Time	YST	Yukon Standard Time
CST	Central Standard Time	AST*	Alaska Standard Time
MST	Mountain Standard Time	HST*	Hawaiian Standard Time

*Alaska Standard (AST and Hawaiian Standard (HST) are two hours apart during Daylight Savings time. Because Hawaii does not observe Daylight Savings, AST and HST become one hour apart during Standard Time.

These zones extend through the Bahamas, Bermuda, Canada, Caribbean Islands, Mexico and the United States. Canada also has Newfoundland Standard Time (NST). Daylight savings time is standard time moved forward how to provide an additional daylight hour in the evening. Example: 8:00 p.m. CST becomes 9:00 p.m. NST. Daylight savings time extends from the beginning of April through the end of October. Conversion dates, standard to daylight and daylight to standard, are used by airlines for inaugurating summer and winter flight schedules.

Universal Time Coordinated (UTC) and the International Date Line

When people express time, they generally speak in terms of local time. International airlines deal with many time zones, and communication of time can be difficult. To eliminate confusion, a common time measurement was established; the Universal Time Coordinated or UTC (previously known as Greenwich Mean Time or GMT).

Imagine the world as a circle. A cycle has 360 degrees. There are 24 time zones throughout the world with each time zone consists of 15 degrees. Twenty-four time zones multiplied by 15 degrees for each time zone equals 360 degrees, the Earth. Each country within a time zone adopts standard time convenient to that country. When one travels east of Greenwich, England (or from anywhere in that longitudinal zone) each zone entered to the east is an increase of one hour to UTC. Similarly, each time zone entered to the west of Greenwich, England, is a decrease of one hour to UTC. Airlines that fly internationally use UTC to standardize time for worldwide operation. UTC is used in the flight deck and will be the times you record in your flight logbook and payroll sheets. UTC is recorded as a 24-hour clock. International schedules are printed in local time, but preceding each city or airport is that location's hour plus or minus from UTC. Another demarcation is the International Date Line (IDL) which generally follows 180 degrees longitude approximately halfway between Honolulu and Tokyo, Japan. Countries west of this line are a day ahead of those east of the line.

Flying over the International Date Line:

WEST	***IDL***	***EAST***
Monday	Monday	Sunday
0002 UTC 0102	UTC	0202 UTC
A day is lost		A day is gained

Flying a day west is lost time, but some is regained as time zones are crossed. Flying a day east is gained time, but some is lost as time zones are crossed.

★ ★ ★

13. Exploring New Ground

As a ripple effect of the global meltdown, the airline industry has had to streamline itself. The loss making state-owned AI has introduced a Voluntary leave scheme; open to employees in non-operational areas, that will allow them to opt for leave without pay for 3-5 years. Losses in the current scenario will be sizeable, therefore, mergers and trimming seems to be inevitable future trend. In the U.S, there is a 'Forewarn act' that employees have time for planning their future, even for those on probation or on contract. Even outplacement services can be hired by corporates to ease the transition for the retrenched workforce.

Skills that have already been developed *i.e.,* personal grooming, ability to handle various customers patiently, communication skills, expertise in handling systems will come handy in other service sector opportunities. The hospitality sector is booming and will gladly accept experienced manpower, as will travel and tourism avenues, BPO'S etc.

Corporate also have in-house travel consultants as do hotels with their travel desk. Tour operators, both inbound and outbound, have a large volume of travel requirements.

Cruise lines are another lucrative job options offering worldwide travel and international exposure. One can be a guest relation's manager or event manager on board a cruise liner.

GUEST RELATIONSHIP EXECUTIVE

These are the people who facilitate complaints, liaise with corporate and offer instant solutions to irate guests with a smile.

Event Management

It is another interesting option one can branch out into. Social secretary on board a cruise liner is a challenging job, which only experienced staff can dispense. One travels to exotic locales, with cultured company. Food and lodging is free, as is boarding. You get to travel on comfort, and it's a paid holiday, interacting with various cultures and nationalities! You wine and dine endlessly and make great contacts along the way, which can end rewardingly depending on your networking skills.

Airport Management

It is an entirely new job opportunity and requires prior experience in people-handling skills. It is a Government paid job with after-service benefits. There are shifts involved and carries tremendous responsibility.

- ***Cabin Crew Scheduling Officers:*** This is an airline job and responsibilities include keeping track of flying hours of crew, their medical updates, arranging pick-up, drop or routine transportation, providing information about leave etc.
- ***Flight Dispatch Officials:*** They work in shifts and see to the smooth operations of crew checking, sign in and out forms, liaising with customs and immigration for crew handling, meal allowances etc. This is an airport-based job and they have to handle any 'no shows' of crew and getting crew (operations and cabin) in time to the aircraft, so that no delays occur, as online stations, stopovers and turnarounds, they have to make arrangements for smooth handling.
- ***Ground Staff:*** This again is as skill, airport-based job and requires stamina and people skills to take care of VIP'S and special-need passengers. Checking at counter inside the airport baggage and overweight charges, pets to be carried, reissuing boarding passes, final head count and completing documentation as required by the Civil Aviation authorities and airlines too, is all part of their job. They are the face of the airline for the passengers and command respect. This is a challenging job, very interesting and never boring. You get to interact with celebrities and international personalities. It pays well and with experience, the next step is a supervisor or duty manager's job.
- ***Crew Administration Officer:*** They basically do crew management for the airlines and provide a ready well-trained team, as required for that specific flight operation, *i.e.*, Chinese speaking crew are scheduled to work on a flight that has more people of that particular nationality, to make passenger's feel at home, medical and leave records are maintained. Crew schedules are worked out regularly. They handle man power and movement of operation and cabin crew also.
- ***Flight Training and Instructors:*** They are generally senior cabin crew who take on the responsibility of training and transforming new talent into the finished product, which is a front line job. They have at least 6-8 years of on-hand job experience and fulfill DGCA and airline responsibilities in training in requisite skills. It includes on-hand, theory and familiarisation with all subjects mentioned as mandatory subjects. Their skills rest on honing up the requisite talent and building on positives.
- ***Public Relations Officer:*** This is an executive cadre job, generally prized and high visibility at major offices of the airline. They handle enquiries, irate customers and try to maintain goodwill with corporates, airlines, travel agents, hotels and tour operators. They also issue statements to Press and TV in case of any need.
- ***Sales and Marketing:*** It requires networking, liaisoning with corporate, institutions, hotels and other service providers. They basically sell space on the airline and try and

boost occupancy by focusing on the clients' needs. They may go out of the way to confirm onward reservations, hotel booking, tickets to a concert or a football match, whichever needed by the client.

The marketing team focuses on creating riches for the airline. It creates a brand image and ties up with other airlines, hotels, etc. to promote partnerships, which are mutually profitable to all. It also creates advertising campaigns and incorporates suggestions and feedback from others.

- ***Ticketing and Reservations:*** A transfer can be taken, if done with active flying, but additional skills like IATA/UFTA courses have to be successfully completed. It is a very precision-oriented job, requires one to be familiar with all current rules and regulations regarding fare calculations and international regulations. Though tickets are issued on the computer, reservation and ticketing engine today, one is liable for any mistakes of short collections. In addition, they have to advise passengers which is the best availability of flights for them, on a particular day/airline/sector/class. They also have to advise documentation of passports, visas and health papers etc. required before travel. They sit at the main office of the airline and enjoy unique privileges.

If one has had enough of working with an airline, one can work towards an additional MBA or post-graduate degree, through correspondence, even while flying. It will open up new avenues in a managerial cadre in counselling, training, HR and PR. FMCG companies, consumer durables and malls require experienced staff for interacting with customers to do surveys, assist in complaint handling, wooing customers and even BPO'S.

In a downturn, Indians are known to be survivors and perform beyond expectations when their back is against the wall. Entrepreneurship comes to the fore when you identify the opportunities and work when there is an opening, especially if it's to one's taste. Options like styling salons, opening a new spa/beauty parlour, gift wrapping, bridal consultation are other options.

★ ★ ★

14. Pilots, Co-Pilots, ATCs and AMEs

PILOT/CO-PILOT ASPIRANTS

The aviation industry in India has two distinct sectors: ***Commercial and Military***. Commercial aviation includes passengers airlines and cargo planes, international air services, air taxi and charter operations being major function. Military aviation includes the Indian Air Force and the aviation arms of the Navy and Army. Entry into the flying branch of IAF can be gained by NCC Senior division 'C' Certificate holders or through the National Defence Academy (NDA)/Combined Defence Services Examination (CDS) conducted by the Union Public Service Commission.

Commercial Pilot: The Commercial airlines have typical Organisational structure. This includes airlines operations, maintenance marketing and finance divisions. The job of pilot comes under the airlines operation division.

Career Prospects: A career in aviaton attracts many youngsters, not the least because it offers a glamorous lifestyle and an opportunity to travel around the globe. Job opportunities have multiplied in recent times, since privatisation has resulted not only in a number of private airlines operating in the sector, but new internationl airlines have also started operations in India.

Pilots get lucrative salaries. Add to this the charm of touring the world and going to distant destinations, staying in good hotels, having a status in life and perks of getting free tickets for your family. The charm of flying high-technology machines and soaring high is another factor for the popularity of this career.

It is a highly responsible job with no room for error. Flight timings are unearthly and this will play havoc with your body as well as your family life. If you are medically unfit at any time, you will be grounded with considerable financial loss. Besides that, flying at high altitudes is extremely tiring and may result in reduced vision, slowed reflexes, dizziness and ozone sickness.

THE PILOT LICENCE

Flying at jet speed is adventurous and challenging. If you have a calm demeanour, courage to face challenge (could be anything from bad weather to hijack), ability to stay focussed for long hours and desire to soar like a free bird with nerves of steel, this could be your dream come true. Other desirable traits are: academic qualifications, sound mind in a healthy body, courage and determination, self-confidence and interested to be technologically in step with current aircraft. You have to undergo formal training and obtain a student's pilot license initially, with a flying school that is recognized by Director General of Civil Aviation (DGCA).

The job of a Pilot/Co-Pilot is very challenging as well as rewarding. There are three licenses, which you have to acquire to become a pilot—Student's Pilot Licence (SPL), Private Pilot Licence (PPL) or the Hobby Licence and Commercial Pilot Licence (CPL). A CPL is required for flying as a pilot in any airline.

The Student's Pilot Licence is the first stage of training. SPLs are issued by 23 flying clubs in India. You have to clear an objective written examination, which tests basic mathematics knowledge of the aircraft, engines and aerodynamics. A manual providing sample questions and answers to give an idea about the nature of the questions expected in the examinations is issued by the flying clubs.

The SPL examination is held every month all over India by the flying clubs. Almost every state has a flying club in India.

In addition, the Director-General of Civil Aviation (DGCA) conducts an examination and issues licence for Assistant Flight Radio Telephone Operators (AFR-TO). There is no age limit to acquire a SPL.

The second stage, the **Private Pilot Licence (PPL)**, comprises 60 hours of flying (40 hours with flying instructor & 20 hours solo) after rigorous training under the flying instructor. along with flying (practical) training, you also have to complete a theory curriculum and clear a written examination conducted by DGCA.

This examination tests the student's knowledge about aircraft engines, air navigation, aviation meteorology and seamanship. This, course generally takes two years to complete and makes you eligible for the PPL. Depending upon the availability of a flying instructor and the weather conditions, the period of training may vary.

For the third stage, the **Commercial Pilot Licence (CPL)**, a minimum of 250 hours of flying (including 60 hours of PPL) is necessary. To get a CPL, you need to have the experience of 200 hours of solo flying.

In addition, you have to clear a written examination consisting of subjects like Air Regulations, Aviation Meteorology, Air Navigation, Technical Planning and Communications in Radio and Wireless Transmission.

Further, you have to undergo a medical fitness test conducted by a team of doctors approved by the DGCA and the Central Medical Establishment (CME) of the Air Force Unit. The average period of training for commercial pilot is one year.

In India, the PPL and CPL training is carried out with the help of single engine aircrafts like Cessna and the Pushpak. The acquisition of a CPL is not sufficient. Before you can fly a domestic flight, you must gain experience of minimum 15 hours of solo flying in a multi-engine aircraft.

The pilots after acquiring the CPL, get trained at Hyderabad (Andhra Pradesh) with Indian Airlines. The duration of this training is six months to perfect the technical know-how and flying skills. You learn to be a team player, but a leader who will set examples in conduct and in trying conditions.

Air India recruits Trainee Pilots on the basis of Written Test, Psychometric Test, Personal Interviews and Simulator Flight Proficiency Test (SFPT). Those who clear the Written Test are called for further tests and interviews.

The fee of flying per hour is different for the various flying clubs across different States due to variations in the operational costs.

On an average, the total cost of getting trained as a pilot is about Rs. 10 lakh to Rs. 11 lakh in India. If you have been trained abroad and intend to work in India, you are required to take an examination called Composite Written Examination conducted by DGCA. Besides, you have to appear for a one hour day and night flying each, under the Chief Flying Instructor.

There are many options for doing this in 4 months / 6 months abroad but the cost is exorbitant. (which can be recovered in a few years as the salary is very high for pilots.) The career has a long span and it's a very prestigious job. The retirement age varies with airlines.

There is urgency for the recruitment of pilots as the aircrafts are increasing in number day by day. As per the statistics, the country would need 15,000 pilots by 2020.

Recruitments are done directly for airlines and charter companies or those preferring private pilots for personal fleet, through advertisements, on a regular basis. Foreign airlines too recruit internationally. UK, US and Europe are all lucrative options. However, a pilot needs to be licensed to fly in that country, after completing DGCA requirements, including flying hours, number of take-offs and landings in a variety of a aircraft.

Aptitude: There are certain attributes to be a Pilot. First of all, one should not be afraid of heights and should have a passion to fly those machines. One should possess a good coordination of mind and limbs. The ability to remain calm under any circumstance and apply theoretical knowledge into practice while flying is very important.

A Pilot has to be quick thinker as he is the one who is responsible for the lives of many. One should have patience, commitment, responsibility and self-confidence. A lot of hard work, stamina, adaptability to follow difficult time schedules, good team spirit etc., are also required in an aspirant. Most importantly, one must have emotional stability in crisis situations.

Eligibility: To become a Pilot/Co-Pilot, one should have the licence of SPL for which matriculation and 16 years of age is prescribed for appearing for the test. To get a CPL, one should have passed 10+2 examination with Physics and Mathematics and must be between the age of 18-30 years. The minimum height should be 5 feet and eyesight 6/6.

Remuneration: Sky is the limit for hard working people in Aviation. A trainee Pilot or Co-Pilot, in about 2-3 years, after flying 2000-3000 hours, can become a Flight Commander. A Pilot can earn more depending on the experience, company and the kind of planes they fly.

SOME INSTITUTES OFFERING-PILOT/CO-PILOT TRAINING

- **American Flyers** (India) Pvt. Ltd. 37 Virwani Industrial Estate, Western Express Highway, Goregaon, Mumbai-400063 (Maharashtra).
- **Amritsar Aviation Club,** P.O. Rajasansi, Amritsar Aerodrome, Amritsar (Punjab).
- **Assam Flying Club,** Guwahati Airport, Guwahati-781007 (Assam).
- **Bihar Flying Institute,** Civil Aerodrome, Patna (Bihar).
- **Bombay Flying Club,** Juhu Aerodrome, Santa Cruz (West), Mumbai-400049 (Maharashtra).
- **Carg Aviations** Limited, Hangar No. 3, Civil Aerodrome, Kanpur (U.P.).
- **Delhi Flying Club** Ltd., Safdarjung Airport, New Delhi-110003.
- **Flying Club,** Civil Aerodrome, Indore (M.P.).
- **Government Aviation Training Institute,** Civil Aerodrome, Bhubaneswar (Orissa).
- **Government Flying Club,** Aerodrome, Faizabad (U.P.).
- **Gujarat Flying Club,** Civil Aerodrome, Hasni Road, Vadodara-390006 (Gujarat).
- **Hissar Aviation Club,** Textile Road, Sirsa Bypass, Hissar (Haryana).
- **Karnal Aviation Club,** Kunjpura Road, Karnal, Haryana.
- **Ludhiana Aviation Club,** Civil Aerodrome, P.O. Sahnewal, Ludhiana (Punjab).
- **M.P. Flying Club,** Bhopal Civil Aerodrome, Bhopal (M.P.)
- **Nagpur Flying Club,** Sonegaon Aerodrome, Nagpur (Maharashtra).
- **Northern India Flying School,** Jalandhar Cantonment-144005, Punjab.
- **Patiala Aviation Club,** Patiala-147001, Punjab.
- **Rajasthan State Flying School,** Sanganer Airport, Jaipur (Rajasthan).
- **Tata Nagar Aviation** Private Limited, 2 North East Circuit House Area, Jamshedpur-831001 (Jharkhand).

Options Post Flying: There is a ground instructor's job in different fields including air safety and regulations performance, etc. Air force background can also work for a lateral entry.

Options for CPL holders (besides airlines): They are encouraged to join the Coast Guard or Defence or Paramilitary forces like BSF (Border Security Force).

AIR TRAFFIC CONTROLLERS (ATCs)

Air traffic controllers are responsible for maintaining the safe and orderly movement of aircraft along major air routes and around airports by giving pilots specific instructions and advice as to height, speed and course.

The majority of air traffic controllers work in control centres and are responsible for keeping aircraft flying safely through the airways. Others work as approach controllers dealing with aircraft movement into and out of the airport, or aerodrome controllers guiding aircraft through landing and to the terminal.

Role of Air Traffic Controller

There are more than 5,000 aircraft in a busy airspace every day so the demand for air traffic controllers is increasing year on year. Air traffic controllers have a number of aircraft under their control at any one time.

As an air traffic controller, your day-to-day job involves the following tasks:

- Keeping radio and/or radar contact with aircraft;
- Directing the movement of aircraft *en route* or at an airport;
- Instructing aircraft to climb or descend and allocating final cruising level;
- Providing information to aircraft about weather conditions;
- Making sure that minimum distances are maintained between planes;
- Handling unexpected events, emergencies and unscheduled traffic.

Key qualities include alertness, extreme caution, clear understanding of rules, parameters of his job, awareness of airports support systems and aviation regulatory bodies. Ability to handle stress in an emergency could mean the difference between being alive or dead for passengers in an aeroplane, caught in an emergency.

To become an air traffic controller, you will need to find:

- The right course for you;
- The training options those available to you;
- The National Air Traffic selection process;
- National Air Traffic training course-duration, subjects, exams to be cleared;
- Entry requirements for training courses;
- Your Class 1 medical certificates;
- The different training courses and what to expect;
- How to prepare effectively for the interview;
- Group exercises and what they involve;
- Psychometric testing and what it involves.

The best option is through the Internet, where most information is given. Vacancies for jobs appear in the daily newspapers and when the various institutes offer the training psychometric tests are used by many employers and organisations as a tool to assess potential candidates for a specific job or role. A psychometric test is a way of assessing a person's ability or personality in a measured and structured way.

The tests come in many different forms and it can be extremely difficult to prepare for them effectively. Some tests are used by employers to help them in their recruitment process, while other tests can help people with their career-decision making.

Organizations believe tests help them to recruit the right people with the right mix of abilities and personal qualities. They are also useful for "sifting out" large numbers of applicants at an early stage and so saving the employers both time and money. Tests can be administered by pencil and paper or even by computer. You may even be asked to sit the tests as part of a selection process, at a test centre or even online. Employers usually set a particular score which you need to achieve in order to proceed to the next level.

Prepare Fully for The Tests: Get a good night's sleep before the test and remember to take breakfast. This will go a long way to helping your concentration levels and ultimately improving your scores.

On the morning of the test day, try to avoid stimulating drinks such as coffee as this will only serve to make you jittery and anxious. Drink water instead to help keep your mind clear and focussed.

Don't Panic Before The Tests: Don't panic during the build-up to the tests. Whilst some psychometric tests are difficult, the answer is more often the most obvious and the simplest one.

By panicking both before and during the tests you will only inhibit your intellectual functioning. Try deep and controlled breathing prior to the tests to help calm your nerves. This will also help you to focus your mind on the task in front of you.

It is a proven fact that those candidates who spend 10 minutes controlling their breathing and relaxing, immediately prior to the test have more chances of success.

Practice Makes Man Perfect: Practice makes man perfect and in relation to psychometric testing this statement couldn't be more relevant. Take the time to practise sample test questions and one can improve actual test scores on the test day.

Psychometric Testing

- Verbal comprehension tests;
- Numerical reasoning tests;
- Mechanical comprehension exercises;
- Spatial reasoning questions;
- English language tests;
- Symbol rotation tests;
- Understanding information tests;
- Selecting the odd one out tests;
- Working hours;
- Reasoning exercises;
- Work rate tests;
- Fault analysis tests;
- Electrical comprehension tests;
- Map reading skills exercises;
- Check letters test;
- Memory tests;
- Distance number tests.

For Indian aspirants, there are many domestic as well as international avenues available for training to be a pilot.

Flight Academy of New Orleans, USA conducts training for Indian students and meets the DGCA requirements.

Minimum Requirements to Enroll: *• 10+2 with Maths and Physics; • For issuance of commercial pilot certificate, applicant must be 18 years of age.*

FLIGHT TIME / TRAINING

Most Indian students require flight time/training as listed below, and institutes are eager to accommodate such training needs.

- 200 hours total time;
- 100 hours of PIC;
- 10 take offs/landings by day and 10 take offs/landings by night in the last 6 months before issue of licence;
- X-country has to be a destination beyond a radius of 100 Nm;
- 1 Day x-country (PIC) with two full stop landings at two airfields other than the airfield of departure, for a minimum of 300 Nm;
- 1 Day x-country check (Instructor on board) for a minimum of 250 Nm with 1 full stop landing at a second airfield (in the last six months before issue of licence);
- 1 Night x-country check (Instructor on board) for a minimum of 120 Nm without landing *enroute* (in the last six months before issue of licence).

INSTRUMENT RATING (IR)

Obtain your instrument rating (IR) per details given below:

- 10 hours of IR flying (Hood or Actual);
- 5 hours can be on an approved Simulator;
- 5 hours on aircraft is mandatory;
- Every flight for IR is dual;
- 10 minutes are calculated towards taxi/take off and taxi in.

MULTI RATING

Obtain your multi rating per details given below with minimum 25 hours to include:

- 15 hours actual flying time;
- 10 hours could be on simulator;

- Minimum 3 hours by night;
- 3 hours test for day/night and instrument check (in the last six months before issue of licence);
- Students should have a multi-engine IFR rating.

Step 1 - Submit admission documents;
Step 2 - Wire admission fees;
Step 3 - Receive acceptance packet;
Step 4 - Get visa interview, if enrolling in an institute abroad;
Step 5 - Visa approval;
Step 6 - Travel to institute where you are accepted.

AIRCRAFT MAINTENANCE ENGINEERS (AMEs)

The Aircraft Maintenance Engineers play a stellar role in Aviation sector as they are the ones who ensure that the aircraft is in a perfect condition before take-off. an engineer needs to be completely focused on safety as the casual attitude can pose a danger to the lives of people on board. The Aircraft Engineer has to certify the aircraft fit for release. The job ensures the availability of safe aircraft at the best possible cost. The Engineering and Maintenance department of an airline performs scheduled and unscheduled tasks, leading to restoration of the expected airworthiness. The job includes diagnostic and mechanical duties covering maintenance, repair, trouble shooting and overhaul, in addition to performing inspection and modification on an aircraft.

Aptitude: An Aircraft Maintenance Engineer, at times, has to work under stringent conditions, tough deadlines and harsh weather in difficult locations. To overcome all this, one should be logical, focused and have perseverance.

Eligibility: The basic and minimum qualification required to be an Aircraft Maintenance Engineer is a Senior School Certificate with Mathematics, Chemistry and Physics as main subjects. Candidates are required to undergo a 3 year certificate course on aircraft maintenance engineering, conducted by various training schools approved by the Director-General of Civil Aviation. Candidates also need to undergo structured aircraft type course in the mechanical or avionics stream and obtain regulatory licences or approvals on a type of aircraft. Candidates need an engineering degree for career in support services in technical services, engineering planning quality assurance and logistics. Courses on structured aircraft type maintenance are also desirable.

★ ★ ★

15. Customer Service Training Procedures

THE Airlines demand superior customer service. The procedures are designed to be convenient and trouble free for the travelling public. It is important that all flight attendants become thoroughly familiar with the contents of this section. By being able to locate needed information, all employees can offer accurate guidance and consistent service to customers.

In the following section, guidelines and procedures to follow are listed. However, each flight attendant, through experience and skills acquired through training, may adapt certain procedures as necessary to meet the situations.

CASTE, CREED OR COLOUR

The Airlines provide equal services to all customers regardless of caste, creed, or colour. If a customer objects to riding with another customer because of caste, creed, or colour, he/she should be advised of the airline's policy and that airlines are required by law to carry all persons who comply with Federal regulations. The customer may be given the option of an immediate refund or making reservations on a later flight.

COMPANY IDENTIFICATION

All Airline employees are issued a photographic identification badge. Employees are required to have their badge ready for presentation when requested. In the event an employee's I.D. badge has been stolen or lost, a replacement badge will cost money. If an employee changes bases or stations, his or her replacement badge will be issued free as long as the old badge is returned.

RECURRENT TRAINING

Each flight attendant is required to attend recurrent flight attendant training once during the twelve-month period following completion of initial training and once every twelve months thereafter. Each flight attendant will be assigned a base month upon completing initial training. Base months will remain the same each year. The only exceptions will be those flight attendants returning from maternity or medical leave of absence or any reason deemed necessary by management. In such cases, the flight attendant will be notified of a new base month assignment. It is the flight attendant's responsibility to verify current flight attendant status.

Test Requirements: Each flight attendant is required to satisfactorily complete recurrent ground training and a competency check. A competency check may include, but is not limited to a written examination, evacuation drills on trainer, fire fighting drills, equipment proficiency check and CPR techniques. Any Flight Attendant not considered by the instructor to have satisfactorily completed Recurrent Training for the second time will be dealt with on an individual basis at the sole discretion of management.

NON-DISCRIMINATION ON THE BASIS OF HANDICAP

The following information and procedures provide guidelines for compliance with regulation and accommodating the needs of disabled customers.

Airlines carriage of disabled customers is governed by the department of transportation.

Definition of a Disabled Individual

The definition of a disabled individual is any person who has a physical or mental impairment that substantially limits one or more major life activities.

Airlines will not discriminate against any otherwise qualified handicapped individual, by reason of such handicap.

Airlines will not refuse transportation to any qualified handicapped person whose appearance or involuntary behavior may offend, annoy or inconvenience crewmembers or customers.

Airlines shall not refuse to provide transportation to qualified handicapped individuals by limiting the number of such persons who are permitted to travel on a given flight.

Transportation of Disabled Customers Complaint Resolution Official (CRO)

The CRO may be an airport service agent, supervisor, assistant station manager, etc. who has received special training in this area. They will have the authority to resolve the complaint. Each station has trained CROs available during operating hours.

Anytime, there is a question regarding the transportation of a disabled individual, or someone on board the aircraft wishes to file a complaint regarding the violator of DOT policies, the CRO should be contacted.

The flight attendant will:

notify the airport service agent;
notify the captain;
fill out a flight attendant report of irregularity.

The airport service agent will:

contact the CRO (the airport services agent may be the CRO).

The captain will:

Discuss any concerns discreetly with the CRO and "A" position flight attendant.

Provisions of Equipment

Airlines do not provide oxygen, transport or accept customers requiring medical oxygen on-board.

Airlines accept incubators and provide hook-up for a respirator to the aircraft electrical power supply. Airlines do not accept a customer who must travel in a stretcher without proper notification from the airport service agent/CRO.

Airlines generally permit qualified handicapped customers using personal ventilators/respirators to bring and use their equipment, including non-spillable batteries, on-board the aircraft.

Wheelchairs are to be checked and placed in the cargo bin with regular bag tags. If disassembly is required for stowage, it is reassembled and returned it to the customer.

At no time may a customer be left unattended in a wheelchair or lift chair for more than 30 minutes.

Many customers wish to be boarded and deplaned in their own wheelchairs. Such passengers must have a regular bag tag and a "Claim at Gate" tag. Their goods is delivered to the stairway upon arrival at the destination.

Assistance Devices

Airlines permit disabled customers to stow canes, and other assistance devices on-board the aircraft in close proximity to their seat. These devices are not considered carry-on items and do not count towards the customers' two carry-on limit.

To Stow an Assistance Device: Under a row of connecting seats, flat on the floor and not protruding into aisle, the device may be stowed in between non-emergency-exit window seats and fuselage. Besides, a device may also be stowed flat on floor not protruding into aisle and on floor of overhead bin.

Assistance Animals

Airlines permit dogs and other assistance animals used by disabled customers to accompany the customers on a flight at his/her seat bastion choice unless the animal obstructs an aisle. The exception is the emergency overwing window exit row(s).

Station personnel may accept as evidence that an animal is assistance animal by...

- Presentation of identification cards;
- Other written documentation;
- Presence of harnesses or markings of harnesses;
- Tags;
- The credible verbal assurance of the qualified disabled customer using the animal.

Guide Dog: To assist the blind or visually impaired, recognized as a dog in harness.

Service Dog or Monkey: To assist paraplegic and quadriplegic customers, recognized as a dog in harness or a caged monkey.

Hearing Dog: To assist the deaf or hearing impaired, hearing dog may wear a blaze orange collar.

Guidelines for Assistance Animals

- A dog should remain with its owner throughout the flight;
- Do not be fearful in approaching assistance dogs, they are taught to accept strangers calmly;
- While a dog is in a harness, they are considered working and should not be touched or petted;
- Discourage children from touching or petting, while it is in his harness;
- Assistance animals may not occupy a seat;
- Service monkeys must remain caged and stowed under seat throughout the flight.

Boarding

With the exception of restrictions involving overwing window exit row(s) seating, airlines cannot:

- Require a disabled individual to occupy a certain seat;
- Require a disabled individual to pre-board;
- Require a disabled individual to sit on blankets.

Certain situations, however, necessitate the pre-boarding of select customers to allow them to be properly accommodated. If assistance is needed an airport service agent is always available to assist pre-boarded customers to the aircraft. He is also available for assistance in making flight connections and transportation between gates. Flight attendants should offer assistance to the airport service agent when possible on boarding and deplaning the aircraft. They should always introduce and identify themselves when offering assistance. They should always ask if assistance is wanted as the person knows best the manner in which he can be assisted.

Seats equipped with moveable aisle armrests are located sporadically throughout the cabin to ease the seating process of disabled customers.

NOTE: The armrest must be in the down position for taxi, takeoff and boarding. In the possible event of an emergency evacuation, it is important to remember where the disabled customers are seated.

Prior to departure, flight attendants must, by regulation, individually brief on emergency procedures, those persons needing special assistance to move to an exit. Additionally, as appropriate to the situation, they must be briefed on smoking, seat belts, seatbacks/tray tables, and flotation devices and on where, when and how to use them.

Flight attendants provide the following cabin services to disabled customers:

- Assistance in moving to and from seats;
- Assistance in preparation for eating (i.e., opening packages and identifying food);
- Assistance in moving to and from the lavatory;
- Assistance in stowing and retrieving carry-on items.

Flight attendants are not required to provide extensive special assistance of the following nature:

- Assistance with actual eating;
- Assistance within the lavatory;
- Assistance at the customers seat with elimination factors;
- Provision of medical services.

Prior to landing, flight attendant should inform the captain of any customer who requires additional assistance at the next station and remind him/her of any wheelchairs needed.

3-Man Assist

This type of assistance is provided to assist movement to or from an on-board wheelchair. Be sure that the red brake bar is down and in the locked position on the wheelchair and that the armrests are up. Take high heels off and squat with knees bent and back flat. Assume proper position as described below with face head, eyes and chin towards the ceiling.

- Person #1 should say "READY" (if you are not ready, please say "STOP") and then "1-2-3 lift". All three lift the person on this cue. To transport once customer is in wheelchair, position arm rests down, secure with velcro strap and unlock brake. Thereafter, return customer to seat using the 3-man assist, and store the wheelchair in accordance with procedures given in the emergency chapter.

- Person #2 is the second tallest. Stand to one side of the wheelchair, place one hand under the customer's thigh and another on the customer's lower back.

- Person #3 is the shortest. Stand In front of the wheelchair, wrap hands behind customers knees and grasp your forearms.

16. Grooming Standards

COMPANY ISSUED UNIFORM GUIDELINES

- Uniforms must be cleaned and pressed before your show time and while away from your base;
- Shirts are to be worn tucked in (except for maternity shirts);
- Uniform items should not be used for personal use;
- Uniforms may not be worn while consuming or purchasing alcohol;
- The original design of the uniform may not be changed. Alterations may be made for proper fit, e.g., hemming, waist diameter etc. This will be accomplished with the uniform fitting company upon receipt of the uniform;
- Upon termination of employment, all company-issued uniform pieces must be returned to the company in good condition;
- Company issued items include: polo style shirts, long pants, shorts, sweater, apron and wings;
- *Shoes:* Plain white leather (no mesh or canvas), low cut or athletic style shoe, mid tops are acceptable (No high tops). No side colours, emblems, or marking (other than white or light gray stitching) of any kind allowed;
- *Hats:* Only ICS logo hats purchased at the ICS store are permitted;
- *Socks:* With tennis (long or short pants);
- Females may wear coloured socks to match exactly the shirts. White socks are acceptable;
- Males must wear only white socks with tennis shoes;
- Crew, bobby sock apes, or tennis types will be allowed, but they must cover the ankle bone (No pom-poms allowed);
- Navy blue socks with Penny loafers (long pants, male or female). White socks with Penny loafers (shorts, male or female);

- *Belts:* Made of leather or leather look; must coordinate with the uniform pants. Woven belts are acceptable;
- Buckle should be leather covered, silver or gold;
- Blue belt with tennis shoes;
- Oxblood belt with penny loafers;
- Shorts may be worn April 1 through October 31 only.

JEWELLERY GUIDELINES

- *Rings:* One on each hand for both males and females is acceptable. Engagement and wedding bands are considered as one;
- *Necklaces:* Short gold or silver chains next to skin acceptable. No necklace out side of wardrobe for either males and females;
- *Bracelets:*
  - ★ Only one (1) allowed; no more than 1/2 inch wide;
  - ★ Must be silver or gold tennis style bracelet;
  - ★ No bangle style bracelets allowed;
  - ★ Medic alert bracelets are permitted;
  - ★ Ankle bracelets are not permitted with uniform.
- Visible body piercing (other than for the ear) is not permitted;
- Earrings no larger than a 50 cent piece are acceptable. Gold, silver, pearl or diamond earrings are preferable. Only two (2) earrings per ear is allowed and both must be in the lobe of the ear, stud or hoop types only. Dangling and ear cuffs are not permitted;
- If a second earring is worn, only gold, silver, pearl or diamond stud is allowed. Males are not allowed to wear earrings.

ADDITIONAL ACCESSORIES/JEWELLERY GUIDELINES

- *Watches:* All ASAP and flight attendants are required to wear a tasteful style watch while on duty;
- *Flashlight (Torch):* All flight attendants are required to purchase their own flashlight and to have reasonable accessibility to it while on duty;
- Flashlights must be able to turn on and stay on (no "push to illuminate" flashlights).
- *Eyewear:* Glasses should be of a tasteful design; lenses or eyewear should be clear, not tinted. Sunglasses are to be worn outside only;
- *Name Badges:* Company issued wings must be worn while on duty on the left side above the company logo;
- ***Belts:*** To coordinate in colour with uniform pants. Made of leather or fabric material. Pins/buttons. Only company approved pins/buttons are allowed.

ADDITIONAL OPTIONAL CLOTHING AND ACCESSORIES

- Luggage may be payroll-deducted;
- Navy parkas may be payroll-deducted;
- Apron (butcher block style);
- Baseball caps purchased only through the company store may be worn inflight.
- Denim uniform shirt (pink) may be payroll-deducted;
- Oxblood penny loafer shoes—Bass, dexter, or approved by supervisor;
- Nylon jacket.

PERSONAL HYGIENE AND APPEARANCE GUIDELINES

Undergarments: All male and female employees are expected to wear appropriate undergarments. Females must wear a bra.

***Make-up*:**

- *Females:*
  Make-up consists of foundation, blush, mascara and lipstick and is to be used so agent presents a natural, wholesome appearance with no garish or over-done effects. Never apply make-up in public;
- *Males:*
  Are not permitted to wear make-up;
- *Fragrances:*
  Perfumes, colognes, and after-shaves should be used in light scents and sparingly.

Nails:

- *Females:*
  A) Cleaned and well-shaped at all times;
  B) Not to exceed 3/4" length from the cuticle to the end of the nail;
  C) Nails must be same length on both hands;
  D) Shade of polish must blend with uniform. Polish may not be peeling or chipped;
  E) Decals and gold nails are not permitted.
- *Males:*
  A) Kept clean and trim;
  B) Length should not extend passed the tip of the finger;
  C) Colored polish is not permitted.

★ ★ ★

17. Pre-flight Duties upon Boarding the Aircraft

Introduce Yourself

Time permitting; Introduce yourself to the flightdeck crew.

Stow your luggage in one of the following places:

- Forward overhead bin ("A" Position only);
- Aft overhead bin;
- Aft galley stowage compartment;
- Under the last row of seats.

Check overall cabin appearance/cleanliness;
Seat belts crossed;
Seatback pockets free of trash;

Each seatback pocket/literature pocket should contain:

- Safety information card;
- Inflight magazine;
- Airsickness bag;
- Tray tables clean and upright;
- Seatbacks upright;
- Overhead bins opened;
- Air vents opened;
- Adjust cabin appearance/cleanliness if needed;
- Perform cabin security check.

"A" POSITION

- Coordinates with captain and airport services agent to determine pertinent customer and flight information;
- Briefs "B" and "C" flight attendants on any pertinent customer or flight information. Sets entry and cabin lights to full bright for boarding;
- Pre-flight checks EMK and PA system.

Checks forward galley for supplies:

- Serving tray;
- Drink order pads;
- Beverages;
- Beginning inventory of liquor and beer kit;
- Peanuts and other snacks;
- Nothing stowed in area marked "No Stowage";
- Check operation of coffee pot and that it is empty.

Secure Forward Galley

Securing the galley consists of:

- All doors, cabinets, and kits closed and latched. Coffee pots latched;
- Absolutely nothing left unsecured on the floor or blocking access to entry or galley doors;

  Check forward lavatory for cleanliness, supplies, and fire threats. Ensure that the following items are there in the plain:
- Paper towels;
- Toilet paper;
- Kleenex;
- Soap;
- Ensure fwd lav spring loaded trash flap is operative;
- Check the forward jumpseat, seat belts and shoulder harnesses for proper operation. If the jumpseat does not automatically retract, notify Captain;
- Coordinate with "B" and "C" flight attendants regarding any missing supplies, equipment, or cabin discrepancies and advise the Captain and/or airport services agent;
- Communicate any cabin discrepancies found to the captain.

"B" POSITION

Checks aft galley for the following supplies:

- Two serving trays;
- Drink order pads.

Beverages:

- Beginning inventory of liquor, beer and wine kits;
- Peanuts;
- Snacks (when applicable);
- Nothing stowed in area marked "No Stowage";

- Check operation of coffee pots and that they are empty;
- All doors, cabinets, and kits closed and latched.
- Coffee pots latched;
- Absolutely nothing left unsecured on the floor or blocking access to entry or galley doors;
- Check water quantity using water gauge;
- Check aft lavatory for cleanliness, supplies, and fire threats;
- Paper Towels
- Toilet paper;
- Kleenex;
- Soap;
- Ensure aft lav spring loaded trash flaps are operative;
- Check aft equipment;
- Contents of flight attendant pouch;
- Biohazard kit;
- Check the aft jumpseat, seat belts and shoulder harnesses for proper operation. If the jumpseat does not automatically retract, notify captain;
- Inform "A" flight attendant of any supplies missing or cabin discrepancies;
- Pre-flight check emergency light switch.

"C" POSITION

Checks all cabin equipment included on the cabin equipment checklist and reports to "A" position flight attendant/captain, all equipment is okay or any discrepancies so the captain can take appropriate action.

Aircraft with aft facing seats at the overwing:

- Ensure that the only items in the overwing holder is the safety information card. Stowage of sickness bags, magazines and promotional material is not allowed in the holder.
- Inform "A" flight attendant of any cabin discrepancies.

18. Emergency and Security

For references throughout an aircraft manual, the captain's side of the aircraft will be referred to as aircraft left and the first officer's side of the aircraft will be referred to as aircraft right. In addition, galley doors may be referred to as service doors.

Emergency Exits

There are 8 emergency exits:

- 2 sliding windows in flightdeck—1 aircraft left and 1 aircraft right;
- Forward entry door;
- Forward galley door;
- 2 overwing window exits—1 aircraft left and 1 aircraft right;
- Aft entry door;
- Aft galley door.

All exits are plug type. All exits may be opened from the outside as well as the inside, with the exception of the sliding window beside the captain.

Door Exits

All doors are equipped with door mounted slides:

- A red strap is located above each window on all doors to indicate an armed and disarmed door slide;
- All slides are designed to inflate automatically;
- All door handles rotate aft;
- All doors will open forward towards the flight deck.

To arm a slide (prior to pushback) stairway is moved away from aircraft:

- Flight attendant announcement: "Flight attendants prepare doors for pushback;"
- Place strap across door window indicating an armed slide;
- Remove girt bar from the door brackets and place it in the floor brackets;
- Door exits are in emergency mode;

Captain turns off "Fasten Seat Belt" sign:

- Flight attendant announcement "Flight attendants prepare doors for arrival;"
- Remove the girt bar from the floor brackets and place it in the door brackets;
- Place strap in position above door window indicating a disarmed slide;
- Door exits are in normal operation mode.

To Open a Door in Emergency Mode

Face door and assess conditions. If conditions are found to be poor, do not open! Block exit and redirect customers to a safe, usable exit and if conditions are clean then:

- Place one hand on door assist handle;
- Place other hand on door handle;
- Rotate door handle in the direction of the arrow. Door swings in and then out;
- Transfer hand to assist handle;
- Push the door open completely against the aircraft-slide which should inflate;
- If slide does not inflate, pull inflation handle as back up to ensure slide inflates;
- Evacuate customers.

To Open an Overwing Window Exit in Emergency Mode

Face aft and assess conditions. If conditions are poor, do not open! Block exit and redirect customers to a safe, usable exit and if conditions are clear, then:

- Remove plastic cover when present;
- Place aisle hand in the top hand hold;
- Place other hand palm-up in the bottom hand hold (or grasp arm rest);
- Pull down on top hand hold/handle to remove window;
- Stow window on seats (in some circumstances, it would be preferable to throw window outside aircraft, away from exit);
- Evacuate customers.

On some 300 series aircraft, a plastic cover is present over the top hand hold and release handle. This cover must be removed before the exit can be opened. A bottom hand hold/ release handle or an arm rest will also be present to aid in manoeuvering the opened window outside and away from the aircraft.

CABIN EQUIPMENT PRE-FLIGHT CHECKLIST

Is it there? Will it operate? Is it secure?

The cabin equipment checklist consists of:

- Aft closet fire extinguisher (if applicable);
- Flight deck key;
- H_2O extinguisher;

- Emergency medical kit;
- On-board wheelchair;
- Emergency light switch;
- P.A. microphones;
- Biohazard kits;
- Halon extinguishers;
- Lavatory fire extinguishers;
- First aid kits;
- CPR masks;
- Boxes of latex gloves;
- Seat belt extensions and demo masks;
- Megaphones;
- P.B.E.s;
- Emergency flashlights;
- Door slide gauges, red strap above each door window and girt retaining straps, where applicable;
- P.O.B.s.

GENERAL SECURITY PROCEDURES

Security procedures and policies have been established to provide a safe environment for our customers, flight crews, and airport employees. The following procedures and policies are issued in confidence and should not be discussed with persons other than crewmembers. It is the responsibility of all Airline employees to ensure the security programme is followed. Through observations and alertness, many threatening situations can be prevented.

Employees/Crew Members Identification Badges

- All Airline employees are issued photo identification badges;
- Employees should have their I.D.s in their possession during the following times:
  - ⋆ When on duty;
  - ⋆ At company facilities;
  - ⋆ When using company passes or privileges;
  - ⋆ I.D.s must be shown upon request.
- Crew members are not required to wear their I.D. while working on the aircraft, however, anytime a crew member is in a secured, non-public area (i.e. stairway, ramp) their I.D. must be worn visible at waist level or above.

Ground Security

A ground security programme has been established to prevent persons from sabotaging the airport, aircraft or a flight. All aircraft must be closely guarded while on the ground.

Ramp areas must be kept free of sightseers, visitors and other unauthorized persons. Employees are urged to be aware of any suspicious persons observed around the aircraft.

If a suspicious person is noticed you should:

- Approach the person and ask them to show proper identification;
- If proper identification cannot be shown, notify a ground operations supervisor or a customer service supervisor;
- The supervisor will notify airport security as necessary.

TERMINAL SECURITY PROCEDURES

Screening of Passengers at Security Checkpoint

Safety rules require all enplaning customers and visitors (including those travelling non-revenue) to be screened at a security checkpoint before proceeding to the gate area. This screening is normally accomplished through the use of metal detectors.

Screening Qualified Handicapped Customers at Security Checkpoints

Qualified handicapped customers may proceed through the metal detector, and be subject to the same security requirements as other customers. Possession of a mobility aid used for independent travel will not subject the person, or the aid, to special screening procedures if the person or the aid clears the security system without activation. This does not prohibit security personnel from examining a mobility aid or assistive device which, in their judgement, may conceal a weapon or other prohibited items. Private screening will be conducted upon the request of the individual.

Screening Carry-on Baggage

All carry-on baggage passing through the screening point must be inspected physically or with an X-ray device. Articles cleared by this inspection may pass the screening point and be carried into the aircraft cabin. Should a customer refuse to permit the inspection of any hand-carried articles, such articles will not be transported.

Screening Crewmembers and Crewmember Luggage

Working and deadheading crewmembers and luggage must be screened at a security checkpoint before proceeding to the gate areas.

Deadly and Dangerous Weapons

It is a crime for a customer or crewmember to carry an unauthorized, deadly or dangerous weapon, either concealed or unconcealed, aboard an aircraft. Airport security may remove certain items considered to be a deadly or dangerous weapon from a customer or crewmember attempting to pass through a security checkpoint.

Items Considered Deadly or Dangerous

Firearms:

- Any weapon from which a shot may be fired by the force of an explosion including starter pistols, compressed air or BB guns, and flare pistols;
- They also include sabers, swords, hunting knives, souvenir knives, martial arts devices, and such other knives with blades 4 inches long or longer and/or knife considered illegal by local law.

Bludgeons: Blackjacks, clubs, or similar instruments.

Explosives/Ammunition, Flammable Liquids: These include any explosive or incendiary components which by themselves, or in conjunction with other items, can result in an explosion or fire. For example, explosive materials, blasting caps, fireworks, gasoline, other flammable liquids, ammunition, etc., or any combination of these items (generally referred to as a "bomb").

Disabling or Incapacitating Items: All tear gas, mace, pepper spray, chemicals and gases, whether in pistol canister, or any other container, and other disabling devices such as electronic stunning/shocking devices.

Other Articles: Such items as ice picks, straight razors, and elongated scissors, even though not commonly thought of as a deadly or dangerous weapon, but could be used as a weapon, including toy or "dummy" weapons or grenades.

ACCESS TO AIRCRAFT

Jetways provide access to and from the aircraft and are considered secured areas. Jetway doors must remain locked except during customer boarding and deplaning to prevent unauthorized persons from having access to the aircraft. Unauthorized or unbadged persons exempting to enter the jetway or aircraft MUST be tactfully, but firmly, refused entrance into a secured area or boarding of the aircraft.

Each day, the flight attendant faces many challenges of crewing an environment that makes our customers feel welcome and comfortable during their flights, while maintaining a safe and secure atmosphere for their travel. Because inflight careers flight attendants are committed to our customers, “comfort and safety,” he/she must possess a diverse combination of skills, talent and knowledge.

Inflight Careers Airlines provide a three flight attendant cabin crew on all Boeing 737 aircraft. The flight attendant positions are referred to as “A”, “B” and “C”. While each flight attendant has specific duties, it is the “A” position flight attendant who is ultimately responsible for ensuring quality inflight service and for completing all administrative details assigned. This includes such duties as crew communication and coordination, customer announcements, assurance of cabin safety procedures, and communication with scheduling as necessary.

To comply with flight attendant duty and rest requirements, inflight careers may schedule an additional flight attendant to fly the "D" Position. The purpose of this chapter is to provide a set of guidelines consistent with FAA regulations and company policy for reroute procedures. In conjunction with these guidelines, each flight attendant should be able to make sound decisions regarding safety, customer service, and scheduled operations.

ITEMS REQUIRED FOR YOUR FLIGHT

In accordance with the FAA and company policy, it is necessary that all flight attendants ensure that prior to leaving home for their trip...

- They are in complete regulation uniform;
- They have an updated flight attendant Manual;
- They have their company I.D.;
- They have a working flashlight;
- Airport ID.

CHECK-IN PROCEDURES

- Find the captain and introduce yourself to all of the crewmembers. Remain in the check-in area. Check your mailbox for company correspondence (i.e. revisions, bulletins or supervisor memos).

  One hour prior to departure, check in with crew members. Each base has permanent placement for latest manual revisions/bulletins. It is each flight attendant's responsibility to ensure the updating of their manual.

  Read briefing book as required prior to each sequence flown to update yourself on all memos regarding policy and/or procedures.

  Check-in with a supervisor when requested and present the following:

  — Your updated flight attendant Manual;
  — Working flashlight;
  — Company I.D.

  A supervisor may check your personal appearance to ensure it meets the grooming standards.

  Introduce yourself to other flight attendants on your sequence. The "A" Position flight attendant ensures a preflight briefing takes place. The preflight briefing should include:

- Remind "B," "C," and "D" flight attendants to check the status of their manuals to ensure they are up-to-date. Review any special inflight service procedures and pertinent information regarding sequence. This information may be found in your briefing book or mailbox.

GATE PROCEDURES

- At your field or base, be on the aircraft or at the gate minutes prior to departure;
- Keep abreast of the changes pertaining to your flight (i.e. delays, gate changes, cancellations);
- Remain accessible to scheduling in the event of a schedule change;
- Enter the jetway as a group;
- Ensure jetway door closes completely after entering;
- Flight attendants are permitted to leave their luggage unattended in a jetway provided the jetway door is closed and locked. If a jetway door is open/unlocked due to boarding or deplaning, at least one flight attendant must remain with the luggage;
- Coordinate with your crew on hotel "lobby" time with consideration of travel time from hotel to gate.

★★★

19. General Information For Respiratory Problems

Normal Heart and Lungs Anatomy and Function

The heart, a muscle about the size of a clenched fist, is located in the centre of the chest behind the breastbone (sternum) and in front of the spine. It has four valves that regulate the flow of blood through four heart chambers and into the pulmonary artery and the aorta.

The function of the heart is to pump blood to the lungs, where it picks up oxygen, and then sends to the rest of the body. Oxygen is required by all cells of the body to carry out their normal functions. When the heart stops (cardiac arrest), oxygen is not circulated and the oxygen stored in the brain and other vital organs is depleted very fast.

The lungs are basically air sacs surrounded by capillaries. Nerve impulses from the brain to the chest muscles and the diaphragm cause a person to breathe.

As the air sacs fill with air, the blood around them picks up oxygen from the air and carries it back to the heart, which pumps it throughout the body. When air is inhaled, only 1/4 of the oxygen gets taken up by the blood; the rest it exhaled. This is why mouth-to-mouth breathing can provide the victim with enough oxygen (about 16% of the rescuers' breath) to help prevent biological death.

Respiratory Arrest

Respiratory arrest occurs when breathing stops. The heart may continue to pump blood for several minutes, carrying existing stores of oxygen to the brain and the rest of the body. Rescue breathing, a gradual procedure which provides artificial respiration, must be administered to keep the lungs supplied with oxygen. Prompt rescue efforts for the victim of respiratory arrest or choking (foreign body airway obstruction) can prevent death.

Cardiac Arrest

Cardiac arrest occurs when the heart stops beating. Cardiopulmonary resuscitation (CPR) should be administered immediately. CPR is a manual procedure which combines artificial respiration and artificial circulation to keep blood circulating and carrying oxygen to the brain, heart and other parts of the body.

Causes of Sudden Death

Every flight attendant training programme carried out by the airlines, has the CPR training component as part of the mandatory training curriculum. Sudden death can happen to anyone at any age. Some common causes are:

- Respiratory distress;
- Heart disease;
- Drug overdose;
- Smoke inhalation;
- Drowning;
- Electrocution;
- Trauma;
- Allergic reaction;
- Choking;
- Suffocation;
- Inhalation/ingestion of a chemical.

Clinical Vs Biological Death

Clinical death means that the heart-beat and breathing have stopped. This is best thought of as near or apparent death and may be reversed. ("Sudden death" is abrupt or unexpected clinical death). Biological death is permanent brain death due to lack of oxygen. This death is final.

Administering CPR during the first few minutes of clinical death may return the victim back to productive life. Without CPR, biological death will occur. When CPR is started within 4 minutes, the victim's chances of surviving are four times greater than if the victim did not receive CPR until after 4 minutes. Speed in starting CPR is key in saving lives.

CPR Mask/Latex Gloves

When performing rescue breathing, CPR, or the Heimlich manoeuver, latex gloves should always be worn and both CPR masks be readily available. Two CPR masks, along with two boxes of latex gloves (100 gloves per box), are provided on all aircraft. The masks are contained in a plastic drawstring bag. The latex gloves and masks are secured with the Velcro stripping securing the First-Aid kit. The masks and gloves are considered part of the cabin equipment checklist, but are not considered a "NO GO" item.

If masks and gloves are not on an aircraft, fill out a flight attendant report of irregularity and obtain the missing item from a provisioning agent at provisioning city.

Instruction for Use: Prior to using the CPR mask, remove the instruction ring from the seal easy cushion mask. Removing the instruction ring will allow you to make a better seal with the mask. These can be used for a child, adult or infant.

Open the victim's airway and place the assembled mask over victim's nose and mouth. Align the opening of the CPR mask with the victim's open mouth. Apply pressure with your hand to create a complete seal. If a leak is detected, simply reposition your hand until you obtain a complete seal. When a victim has a beard or moustache, obtaining a good seal may be more difficult.

Portable Oxygen Bottle (POB)

Portable Oxygen Bottles (POB) are available for use as needed. Two bottles are secured in the forward right overhead bin, one bottle is secured in mid-cabin right overhead bin, and one bottle is secured in the aft right overhead bin. Refer to the flight attendant manual, emergency chapter for instruction on use of the POB.

RESCUE BREATHING PROCEDURES

Adult/child/infant

- Check for consciousness;
- Gently shake and shout, "Are you okay?";
- Call for help;
- Flight attendant brings POB, CPR masks, and gloves;
- Notify the captain;
- If victim is in seat, place on floor, face up;
- Open airway;
- Head tilt/chin lift (infant-neutral position);
- Check for breathing (5 seconds);
- Look, listen and feel;
- Give 2 breaths (infant-puffs), if no breathing;
- Give breaths slowly and stop when you see chest starting to rise;
- Check for pulse/breathing (5 seconds);
- Adult/Child carotid artery (neck);
- Infant brachial artery (inside of upper arm).

Has Pulse/No Breathing

Begin rescue breathing

- Adult–1 breath every 5 seconds;
- 12 Cycles = 1 minute;
- Count 1 one thousand, 2 one thousand, 3 one thousand, 4 one thousand B-R-E-A-T-H-E;
- Child/infant–1 breath every 3 seconds;
- 20 Cycles = 1 minute;
- Count 1 one thousand, 2 one thousand;
- B-R-E-A-T-H-E;
- Recheck pulse/breathing after 1 minute (5 seconds).

Has Pulse/Has Breathing

Administer oxygen, monitor pulse/breathing each minute thereafter.

CPR Change over procedure—one rescuer CRP

- Should the first rescuer administering CPR become exhausted, a 2nd rescuer can relieve them. The first rescuer should complete at least 4 cycles of CPR before attempting to "change over".
- The "change over" should occur after the completion of a compression/breath cycle.
- The first rescuer will start the cycle with compressions by stating, change, 2, 3, 4, 5...15. Give 2 breaths. Recheck pulse/breathing.
- The 2nd rescuer should kneel next to the victim on the opposite side of the first rescuer and position hands to start chest compressions.
- If no pulse/no breathing, the 2nd rescuer should continue CPR starting with compressions.
- If victim HAS PULSE/NO BREATHING, the 2nd rescuer will continue first aid with rescue breathing.

HEIMLICH MANOEUVER

The Heimlich Manoeuver is an emergency procedure for removing a foreign object lodged in the airway that is preventing a person from breathing. It can be performed on all people. Modifications are necessary if the choking victim is very obese, pregnant, adult, child or an infant.

Common Causes

- Trying to swallow large pieces of food that are poorly chewed;
- Drinking alcohol before or during eating;
- Talking excitedly or laughing while eating, or eating too fast;
- Walking, playing or running with objects in the mouth.

Types of Airway Obstructions

- Partial airway obstruction—Good Air Exchange;
- Partial airway obstruction—Poor Air Exchange;
- Complete airway obstruction.

Partial Airway Obstruction—Good Air Exchange

Symptoms

— Red face;
— Can cough forcefully;
— Restricted breathing/wheezing between breaths;
— Possible difficulty in speaking;
— May progress to poor air-exchange.

First Aid

— Loosen collar;
— Try to communicate; ask, "Can you speak?";
— Stay with the person and encourage them to continue coughing;
— Do nothing until it becomes a partial airway obstruction—poor air exchange or a complete airway obstruction.

Portial Airway Obstruction—Poor Air Exchange

Symptoms

— Weak, ineffective cough;
— A high-pitched noise while inhaling;
— Increased respiratory difficulty;
— Possibly hypnosis (turning blue).

First Aid

— Treat as complete airway obstruction;
— Administer Heimlich manoeuver.

Complete Airway Obstruction

Symptoms

— Bluish complexion;
— Cannot speak, breath or cough;
— Clutching at the neck (universal sign for choking: thumb and forefinger of one hand clutching neck);
— Loss of breathing/possible unconsciousness;

First Aid

— Administer Heimlich manoeuver.

SUMMARIES

Complete Airway Obstruction—Conscious (Adult/Child)

- Complete airway obstruction is when a victim cannot speak, breathe, or cough;
- Call for help;
- Flight attendant brings POB, CPR masks and gloves;
- Notify captain;
- Perform Heimlich manoeuver—abdominal thrusts;
- Stand or kneel behind adult or child and wrap your arms around their waist;
- Place thumb side of your fist on the middle of the breastbone (same area as for CPR chest compressions);
- Grasp fist with other hand and give chest thrusts (quick backward thrusts). Give chest thrusts until;
  Object is expelled;
  Victim becomes unconscious;
  You are relieved by qualified medical help.

Complete Airway Obstruction—Conscious (Infant)

- Check for breathing difficulties;
- Call for help;
- Flight attendant brings POB, CPR masks, and gloves;
- Notify captain;
- Give 5 back blows;
- Head lower than the trunk;
- Give 5 chest thrusts;
- Head lower than the trunk;
- Repeat steps until;

  Object is expelled;

  Victim becomes unconscious;

  You are relieved by qualified medical help.

Complete Airway Obstruction—Currently Unconscious (Adult/Child)

- If on giving abdominal or chest thrusts, the person becomes unconscious, lower victim to floor supporting from behind (protect head) and lay face up;
- Call for help;
- Flight attendant brings POB, CPR masks, and gloves;
- Notify captain;
- Do a finger sweep—Hoping action of moving to floor may have dislodged the object. (Child—only if object is visible);
- Open airway and give 2 breaths;
- Give 5 abdominal thrusts;
- Repeat steps until;

  Object is removed by finger sweep;

  Object is expelled;

  You are relieved by qualified medical help.

NOTE: If victim is obese/pregnant, use chest thrusts instead of abdominal thrusts.

Complete Airway obstruction—Unconscious for some time (Adult/Child)

- Check for consciousness;
- Gently shake and shout, "Are you okay?;
- Call for help;
- Flight attendant brings POB, CPR masks, and gloves;
- Notify captain;
- If victim is in seat, place on floor, face up;
- Head tilt/chin lift;
- Check for breathing (5 seconds);
- Look, listen and feel;
- Give 2 breaths, if no breathing;
- If after second breath chest does not rise, return head to neutral position. Retilt head and give 2 more breaths;

- If chest still does not rise;
- Perform the Heimlich manoeuver;
- 5 abdominal thrusts;
- Finger sweep (child—if object is visible);
- If object is not retrieved:
- Retilt and give 2 breaths;
- 5 abdominal thrusts;
- Finger sweep (child—if object is visible);
- Repeat until;

  Object is removed by finger sweep;

  Object expelled;

  You are relieved by qualified medical help.

Complete Airway Obstruction—Unconscious (Infant)

- Check for consciousness;
- Gently shake and shout, "Are you okay?. Call for help;
- Flight attendant brings POB, CPR masks, and gloves and notify captain;
- Place infant on floor, face up;
- Open airway;
- Head tilt/chin lift (neutral position);
- Check for breathing (5 seconds);
- Look, listen and feel;
- Give 2 breaths (puffs), if no breathing;
- If after second breath chest does not rise, return head to neutral position. Retilt head and give 2 more breaths (puffs).
- If chest still does not rise perform Heimlich Manoeuver.
- 5 back blows (head lower than trunk);
- 5 chest thrusts (head lower than trunk); Finger sweep if object is visible. If object is not Retrieved;
- Retilt breaths (puffs);
- 5 back blows (head lower than trunk);
- 5 chest thrusts (head lower than trunk); Finger sweep if object is visible.
- Repeat until:

  Object is removed by finger sweep;

  Object is expelled;

  You are relieved by qualified medical help.

★ ★ ★

20. Getting to Know An Aircraft

MAIN PARTS OF AN AIRCRAFT

For training purposes, normally a Boeing 737 is used. It is a twin engine aircraft used for short to medium range of operations. It can take off and land from airfields with a long range to short range runaway, formerly used by a smaller aircraft.

Its specifications are:

- Two engines;
- Flies for about 1900 miles;
- Has a maximmum speed of 875MPH;
- Seats 138 passengers;
- Flies at an altitude of about 36000 ft;
- Number of crew needed to operate a flight is 5.

The major components of a Boeing are:

— Engine provides the thrust;

— Wings give it "LIFT"; the wingspan here is about 94 ft;

— Tail section gives an aircraft stability and control.

Fuselage is the main body of the aircraft. It consists of the flight deck where all instruments are located that make it work. There is an entry door, openable from inside and outside with a viewer to scan the cabin. A key is often stored in the forward bulkhead to the entry door, as a safety measure, as normally this door should be locked during a flight.

The flight deck is also equipped with two emergency exits; one sliding window at the left and another sliding window at right. Both exits are plug type. The captain's sliding window (aircraft left) is the only exit on the Boeing 737 that cannot be opened from the outside.

CABIN AREA

Equipped with six exits; one forward entry door, one forward galley door, two overwing window exits, one aircraft left and one aircraft right (for emergency use only), one aft entry door, and another aft galley door. Entry doors are located at left. Galley doors are located at right.

AUXILIARY POWER UNIT (APU)

The APU is a gas turbine engine mounted in the tail of the aircraft. This unit, along with the main engines, provides necessary electrical and hydraulic power cabin air conditioning and pressurisation, and heat for wing anti-icing. It operates in the air and on the ground.

However, at engine start-up, all APU air power is used to start the engines. As a result of the pull of power used to start the engine, air conditioning/heating and electrical power temporarily ceases until engines have started. At that time, the APU can resume providing air conditioning/heating and cabin pressurisation.

LUGGAGE/CARGO COMPARTMENT

Two cargo compartment doors, both plug type, are located on the lower right side of the fuselage. The doors can be operated gradually from either the inside or outside of the aircraft. A warning light in the flight deck illuminates when the doors are not closed and locked.

GEARS

- ***Landing Gear:*** The Boeing 737 landing gear, used for taxi, takeoff and landing operations, is a tricycle-type, retractable landing gear consisting of two wheels on each gear.
- ***Main Gear:*** Mounted under the aft portion of the wing, each wheel is fitted with brakes.
- ***Nose Gear:*** Located just forward of the main entry door, nose gear is steerable to provide ground maneuverability; wheels are not fitted with brakes.

ENTRY AND GALLEY SERVICE DOORS

Inward-outward opening plug-type pressure doors are used for all entry doors and galley service doors. This type of door operates on two hinges and uses four roller-type latches for positioning and locking. A light in the control panel will indicate when any door is not locked. Each door has a three-pane window.

The doors may be opened from either inside or outside the aeroplane. The interior door handle rotates easily through a 180 degree arc. The exterior door handle is recessed in the outer face of the door and must be pulled out before it can be rotated. Door opening training is one of the major physical trainings conducted during the cabin crew training programme.

To open the door, movement of either handle rotates a mechanism within the door. This mechanism mechanically lowers the pressure gates at the bottom and top of the door, moves the door into the cabin and then rotates it through its opening to about 45 degrees. From this position, the door is pushed or pulled to the full open position against the airplane fuselage. The door is held in the open position by a mechanical latch on the upper hinge.

To close any of the aircraft doors, the mechanical latch on the upper hinge, referred to as "gust lock", must be depressed. The door is then manually rotated to the aforementioned 45 degree position. From this position, the handle is used to position, close and latch the door. When the handle is rotated to the full closed position, the pressure gates close, sealing the door. Because of cabin pressure loads, these doors cannot be opened during normal flight conditions.

ESCAPE SLIDES

An escape slide is mounted to the inside of each door to be used in an emergency situation for the evacuation of customers and crew.

A pressure gauge on each slide provides a means to ensure the slide is operational.

All slides are designed to inflate automatically when deployed; however, in the case of a malfunction, a red inflation handle will be present as a backup system and may be pulled to manually inflate the slide.

On the slides of some aircraft, there is a quick release handle used to detach the slide from the aeroplane in the event of a water evacuation. This handle which is protected by a cover marked "for ditching" becomes visible once the slide is deployed. On any other aircraft which does not have a quick release handle, the deployed slide may be detached from the airplane by removing the girt bar from the door brackets.

WINDOWS

Rectangular customer cabin windows 10 x 14 inches are located at eye level and are spaced at 20 inch intervals. Each window consists of two panes, each of which being capable to withstanding the full pressure load of the cabin. In addition, a decorative window panel covers each window area to provide protection for the window. Each panel contains opaque sliding window shade eliminating the need for sidewall curtains. The shades slide up to open. These are called Dutch Blinds. Small circular windows are also provided on all entry and galley service doors.

OVERWING WINDOW EXITS

All 737-300 Series aircraft are equipped with two overwing window exits; one aircraft left and one aircraft right. The exits are marked with an exit sign located on the customer cabin ceiling and an exit sign at each overwing window exit approximately two feet above door level. These exits are to be opened only during an emergency evacuation. They may be opened from the inside by pulling down on the top hand hold/release handle.

For ease in viewing outside conditions, a rectangular window and sliding shade, similar to the customer cabin windows, is located at eye level on each overwing window exit. Due to the evacuation mechanism in the exit, however, the window shades slide down to open rather than up.

GALLEYS

Galley units are installed on all Boeing 737 aircraft: one forward and one aft Galleys are stocked with the items necessary to provide a complete in-flight service. In addition, each galley is equipped with an electrical panel containing circuit breakers for various lighting systems and ovens (if applicable).

LAVATORIES

Lavatories are provided on all Boeing 737 aircraft. Each lavatory is equipped with a flushing toilet, a wash basin with hot and cold water, outlets for electric shavers, a fluorescent lighted mirror, a customer call button and information sign, a lavatory service unit, and all necessary toiletry supplies.

Compartments are provided for paper towels, bar soap, Kleenex, sanitary napkins, seat covers, air sickness bags, and toilet paper. A stowage compartment behind the toilet may be used for extra-lavatory supplies.

The door to each lavatory has a slide type door lock which is operated from inside the lavatory. A small sign on the outside of the door will indicate either occupied or vacant, depending on the position of the lock. Locking the door will also illuminate a "lavatory occupied" light on the lower ceiling in the respective cabin area. Although the lock is operated from the inside, if necessary, the door may be unlocked from the outside by inserting a sharp tipped object into the pinhole on the "occupied" sign and sliding it to the "vacant" position. Also, part of the lavatory door is an externally mounted ashtray.

The stainless steel toilets are self-contained units serviced from outside the aircraft. Each lavatory has an independent waste system. The toilet waste is stored in a toilet tank in each lavatory. A separator between the tank and toilet bowl prevents customers from seeing into the tank and liquid in the tank from slashing up into the bowl. The flush handle initiates a cycle in which a chemical-flushing liquid containing dye, disinfectant and deodorant, flows into the bowl from a rotating pump and filtering unit. During ground servicing, the toilet tanks are darned and rinsed, and a chemical liquid is added.

Hot and cold water in each lavatory is provided at a stainless steel sink. The water heater for each lavatory maintains a temperature of approximately 125 degrees F to 133 degrees F. After ground servicing, a new water charge is heated within 4 minutes.

Adjacent to the stainless steel sink is a trash chute with a spring loaded flap door and a removable trash can located under the sink. It is essential that this spring-loaded floor remain "operative" at all times. Periodic checks by flight crewmembers should be conducted to ensure proper operation and for safety checks.

Located near each lavatory on a panel near the sink is a flight attendant call button and a "Return to Seat" customer information sign.

Use of the call button notifies the flight attendants that assistance is needed in the lavatory.

Illumination of the lavatory "Return to Seat" sign notifies that the captain has turned on the "Fasten Seat Belt" sign in the cabin. This sign will remain illuminated until the cabin "Fasten Seat Belt" sign has been turned off.

Also located on the panel is the electric shaver outlet and a razor blade disposal. An air vent outlet is located on the sidewall, just above and to the left of the panel.

Each lavatory is equipped with a smoke detector which is designed to alert crewmembers to the presence of fire. Upon indication, crewmembers should follow prescribed fire fighting procedures.

Each lavatory is equipped with an automatic fire extinguisher. This extinguisher is designed to combat fires that originate in the waste receptacles and sink area.

The water gauge is located over the aft galley door and indicates the amount of water in the tank. When the "PUSH" button on the indicator is pressed, a light illuminates to show the water level. When full, approximately 30 gallons will be available. A shut-off valve is located in the cabinet below the sink in each lavatory. Normally, the drain shut-off valves are ON and the vent valves closed.

Located in the uppermost middle area of the forward and aft galleys, covered by a small panel, is an emergency water shut-off valve. This valve is to be used in the event of an uncontrollable water leak in the galley.

Also located in both forward and aft lavatories is a three-way shut-off valve. This valve may read open/drain/off. In some lavatories, the valve is not readily visible. If it is not, it is located behind a flip latch door, behind the trash can, underneath the sink. If it is difficult to find simply follow the waterline from the sink drain and work backwards to the valve. The valve may also be located out in front, near the trash can, underneath the sink. Once again, the valve is to be used in the event of an uncontrollable water leak.The water heater light when illuminated shows its operating.

OVERHEAD BINS

The overhead bins on each side of the cabin provide stowage for hats, coats, garment bags, briefcases, blankets, and pillows. Each bin is marked with a placard stating the maximum weight of the bin. Articles should not exceed weight limitations for the bin.

CUSTOMER SEATING

Accommodations for 138 tourist-class customers are provided in the delivery configuration. For the most part, the seats will be arranged six-abreast at a typical seat spacing of 3 feet. All seats are equipped with tray tables. The tray tables are attached to and fold into the seat back.

The seats may be adjusted to a maximum recline position of 38 degrees. (Seats immediately forward and aft of partitions or bulkheads do not recline.) The recline button is located on the inner side of the inboard armrests.

In an emergency, the seat cushion may be removed and used as a flotation device.

There is a stowage pocket attached to the back of each seat which contains airsick bags, safety information cards and an in-flight magazine.

CREW JUMP SEATS

A self-folding flight attendant jump seat is located on the aft and forward-facing bulkhead beside the forward and aft entry doors. The jump suits are spring-loaded to the retract position and are fitted with seat belts and harnesses. Safety regulations mandate that each flight attendant jump seat automatically retracts to a stowed position. The seat cushions may also be used as flotation devices. The forward flight attendant jump seat faces aft and the aft flight attendant jump seat faces forward. Both seats accommodate two persons.

CREW LIFE VESTS

Crew life vests may be located behind the actual jump seat itself and not accessible through top stowage type compartments. In this case, the jump seat must be physically removed from the wall in order to preflight or retrieve each vest. The jump seat is secured to the wall by velcro straps and must be properly fitted to the wall after each preflight inspection. Other aircraft jump seats are equipped with an underside compartment that houses each associated life vest. In this case, the compartment must be manually opened to preflight or retrieve the life vest (*).

PASSENGER SERVICE UNIT (PSU)

Service units are provided throughout the aeroplane to supply cooling air, oxygen and electrical services for the customer's and flight attendant's use. These units are fastened to the underside of the overhead bins, overhead and 4-5 inches forward of the seat backs. Each unit contains three air vent outlets, three reading lights with individual buttons, four oxygen masks, a passenger address speaker and one flight attendant call button. There are also "Fasten Seat Belt" and "No Smoking" signs located on the aft face of all units.

CUSTOMER SIGNS

Signs indicating "No Smoking" and "Fasten Seat Belt" conditions are located in the PSU's which insure visibility to all customers. Although the "No Smoking" and "Fasten Seat Belt" signs are contained in one unit, they function independently of each other. A "Return to Seat" indicator is in each lavatory and is visible only when the sign is on. The signs are controlled in the flight deck either manually or automatically. If the captain selects automatic control, all signs will be on when the landing gear is down.

The "Fasten Seat Belt" and "Return to Seat" signs go off when the wing-flaps are fully retracted. During the landing sequence, the "Fasten Seat Belt" and "Return to Seat" signs come on when the flaps are lowered or the landing gear is down. A single low-tone chime sounds over the customer address loudspeaker system each time the signs come on or go off. The "No Smoking" sign stays illuminated during night and while on the ground.

The oxygen masks drop automatically at a cabin altitude of 14,000 feet or may be dropped manually by inserting a pen or small stick into the "pin hole" located at the edge of the compartment.

To manually deploy oxygen masks, the "pin hole" is located in the middle of the PSU.

If no "pin hole" is present, insert an object into the edge of the compartment itself nearest the flight attendant call button.

In the 300 series aircraft, all PSU oxygen masks are connected to a single release lanyard. Pulling down on any mask releases the lanyard and all masks come down. The O_2 generator in that PSU is activated supplying O_2 to the PSU masks. O_2 is generated through the line for approximately 12 minutes and cannot be shut off once the generator is activated.

CREW CONTROL PANELS

There are two flight attendant control panels on all 737 aircraft.

On the 300 series aircraft, the panel is headed directly across from the flight attendant jump seat.

Both flight attendant control panels contain a public address (P.A.) hand-held microphone, a crew interphone, and the "call system" controls. In addition, the forward panel is equipped with the cabin lighting controls, while the aft panel contains the emergency light switch.

FLIGHT ATTENDANT AND DECK OXYGEN UNITS

These units contain two oxygen masks and are recessed in the cabin ceiling above the forward and aft flight attendant jump seats. O_2 will flow through the line for approximately 12 minutes.

As previously stated, the flight deck has a completely separate oxygen system. It is a gaseous, dilute-demand system with four individual masks and regulators for each flight deck crewmember. During the preflight check, the flight deck will switch the oxygen regulator to the 100% position.

PUBLIC ADDRESS SYSTEM (PA System)

Announcements to the cabin are made via the public address system by utilizing the handheld push-to-talk type microphone. An automatic priority system sets the pilot's microphone for first priority.

Call System Controls

The call system controls, located on both the forward and aft control panel, include a captain, fight attendant and reset buttons.

In the customer cabin, there are two different types of call lights secured to the forward and aft lowered ceilings. They are used for communication between the flight deck and the cabin or customer and lav to cabin.

Customer Call to Flight Attendant

The flight attendant call button is located on the underside of each passenger service unit. To call a flight attendant, the customer pushes the call button which illuminates the button in the PSU and the blue master call light located overhead in the forward and/or aft lowered ceiling. A one-toned chime sounds over the public address system. Customer to flight attendant call is cancelled by pressing the button on the customer service unit. The blue call light will be extinguished when all buttons are reset.

Lavatory Call to Flight Attendant

The occupant of the lavatory can call a flight attendant by depressing the flight attendant call button in the lavatory. A high one-toned chime will sounds in the cabin and an amber light will illuminate on the master call unit. The amber light will remain illuminated until the call button has been reset.

On some 300 series aircraft, the reset button is located in the lavatory. Some others have the reset button located on the bulkhead above the flight attendant jump seat, outside the lavatory door.

Captain Call to Flight Attendant

A pilot to flight attendant call illuminates the pink master call lights in the forward and aft lowered ceiling and two-toned chime sounds over the public address system. The lights remain on until the reset button is depressed at the flight attendant's panel.

Flight Attendant Call to Captain/Crew Member

A flight attendant to captain call is made by pushing the captain's call button at any flight attendant control panel. Pressing this button sounds a one-toned chime in the flight deck and illuminates a blue (flight attendant) light on the pilots overhead panel. The blue call light remains on only when a flight attendant to flight attendant call is made by depressing the flight attendant call button on the flight attendant control panel. The pink master call light on the forward and aft lowered ceiling illuminate, and a two-toned chime sounds on the customer address system. The light remains on until the reset button is pressed at either flight attendant control panels. The flight attendants may talk to one another on the handset by depressing the push-to-talk button.

LIGHTING SYSTEM

Cabin Lights

General illumination of the customer cabin is provided by florescent lights in each overhead ceiling panel and above the upper portion of each window panel.

The fluorescent ceiling and window light intensity may be selected as either Bright or DIM. In addition to the fluorescent lights, incandescent night lights are located in the ceiling area to provide a low level of illumination for night flights. All cabin windows and ceiling lights are controlled from the forward flight attendant's panel.

If external power is connected to the aeroplane but is not being used by the pilot, a switch on the forward flight attendant's panel remarked "ground service" may be used to provide a power source for cabin lighting.

Entry Lights

The forward and aft entry areas are illuminated for boarding and departing by incandescent and fluorescent lights in the ceiling, and a threshold light near the door. A switch for the entry light is located on the respective flight attendant panel. Each switch has three positions: Off, DIM and Bright. Light illuminates the threshold when the respective entry light switch is in the Bright position. The entry lights provide dim illumination when ground power is connected regardless of switch position.

Lavatory Lights

Lavatory lighting consists of one fluorescent mirror light and one dome light in each lavatory. The dome light will be on any time power is on in the aeroplane. The fluorescent light is controlled by a micro switch in the door latch. When the door latch is closed, the light will illuminate. When the aeroplane is on the ground, using external power, the fluorescent light will be on regardless of door position.

Exit Lights

In addition to the normal illumination, exit lights are provided in the forward and aft lowered ceiling, above each entry and galley door, and over each of the exit. In addition, lighting on or near the aisle door ensures illumination of the customer escape path. These lights are normally off and will illuminate if a loss of aeroplane power occurs or when the emergency light switch is activated. These lights are powered by self-contained batteries.

Galley Lights

Galley lighting for the forward or aft galley is provided by either fluorescent or incandescent lights beside or above the work area, these are controlled by a switch usually located beside the circuit breaker on the galley. Some aft galleys have additional lighting in the ceiling overhead. This is controlled by a switch beside the water gauge indicator pressurising galley door.

Emergency Light Switch

The emergency light switch, located on the aft flight attendant control panel is to be activated in case all electrical power is lost. It is important to note that a red cover protects the switch and must be lifted before the emergency lights can be turned on.

AIR CONDITIONING AND PRESSURIZATION

Normally, the air which is used for air conditioning and pressurization is supplied by the engines. The auxiliary power unit can also be used to supply air. Air entering the engines or APU is compressed to a high level before it is mixed with fuel and ignited. During compression, the temperature is controlled either automatically or manually by controls on the pilot's overhead panel.

Air flows into the customer cabin through two completely separate compartments.

Conditioned air enters the cabin by way of sidewall ducts to a slotted overhead duct running 70% of the cabin. Part of this air enters the cabin through grills in the light fixtures at either end of the overhead duct.

Air also enters the cabin through individually-controlled outlets in the customer service units and in the lavatories. This air is taken from the cold air side of the air conditioning system and is always colder than the main cabin temperature.

Air exits the cabin through floor level grills in the cabin sidewalls and through vents in the galleys and lavatories. As the air leaves the main cabin, it is routed around the cargo compartments to heat them and out the outflow valves. This process completely exchanges cabin air with outside fresh air, every 2-3 minutes in all of our aircraft.

FORWARD AIR STAIRS OPERATION

The air stairs provide ground access for customer boarding and deplanning. The stairs are cased in the body of the aeroplane directly under the forward entry door and may be operated from either the inside or outside control panel. (Aircraft may or may not be outfitted with an air stair unit).

The interior control panel is located above and to the left of the forward entry door. Operation of the stairs from this position requires that the entry door be opened far enough to provide good visibility of the area below. The open door also releases the air stairs door back pin. This lock pin prevents inadvertent operation of the air stairs while in-flight.

CAUTION: Air stair should not be operated more frequently than three consecutive cycles of normal system operation within a 20 minute period. Air stair should not be operated if winds exceed 40 knots.

A. *Normal Operation Warning:* When operating air stairs from interior control panel, open entry door to cocked position to allow clear visibility of area outside aeroplane to prevent injury to personnel. Do not open door beyond cocked position while operating air stair or equipment may be demaged.

1. *(a)* Crack door open at least six inches to extend the door.

   Caution: Do not release air stair control switch until stairs operating light is extinguished, releasing the air stair control switch before stair extension is complete which could result in jamming of the stairs and structural damage.

(b) Move the "NORMAL" control switch in the "EXTEND" position until the stairs operating light goes out.

Note: The forward air stair control panel is located above the forward entry door.

(c) Pull the upper handrail from the stairs and connect it to fittings inside the aircraft door. The stairs are ready for use.

2. To retract the door—

(a) Disconnect the handrails from their extended fittings and stow them in the handrails ensuring they are in a locked position.

Note: Do not release air stair control switch until stairs operating light is extinguished, releasing the air stair control switch before stair retraction is complete which could result in jamming of the stairs and structural damage.

(b) Move the "NORMAL" control switch in the "RETRACT" position until the stairs operating light goes out.

(c) Close the forward entry door.

B. *Standby Operation:* Flight attendants are required to request permission from the captain to use the standby system for air stairs.

Warning: When operating air stairs from interior control panel open entry door to cocked position to allow clear visibility of area outside aeroplane to prevent injury to personnel. Do not open door beyond cocked position while operating air stair or equipment may be damaged.

AIRCRAFT DIFFERENCES

Each crew member is responsible to be aware of the differences that may be present on any one particular aircraft. A complete preflight check of the aircraft should be conducted to ensure that every crew member has knowledge of these variations. A detailed chart, identifying each aircraft tail (registration) number and associated differences, is found immediately following this section. The following differences may be present on any one particular aircraft.

★ ★ ★

21. Some Facts About Aircraft

MOST POPULAR AIRCRAFT

- Boeing 707 – Popularly known as DC-8 it is the first American built jet liner.
- Boeing 727 – One of the most successful in airlines.
- Douglas DC – 10/Lockheed Tri-Star – One of the first wide bodied aircraft.
- Douglas DC – 9 – Still in service.
- Airbus A300 – The world's first twin engine wide-body airliner.
- Boeing 737 – Best selling civilian plane for airlines.
- Airbus A320 – Pioneer in fly by wire technology.
- Boeing 747 (Jumbo) – The latest airliner between 1968–2005.
- Boeing 777 – Designed entirely by computer.
- Airbus A350 (Superjumbo) – It has 2 full length twin aisles, passenger cabins. It started service with Singapore airlines in October 2007.
- Airbus A380 (Superjumbo) – The world's first twin-deck, twin-aisle aircraft. It began operations in 2009.

MAJOR AIRCRAFT MANUFACTURES

US – Boeing - Douglas (now part of Boeing)
Lockheed (no longer make civilian aircraft)

Canada – Bombardier

Brazil – Embraer

Soviet – Tupolev, Ilyushin

Europe – Airbus industries
ATR-France, Italy
Saab (Sweden)
BAE system (U.K.)

The international market for midsize/jet airliners is now divided between Airbus and Boeing, though Russian manufacturers still sell significant numbers of their products in traditional markets. Smaller-sized ones are AIR/Embraer Boeings and Bombardiers.

AIRCRAFT VALUES

Aircraft	YEAR Built	2010
A330-200	2000	$52.7
A330-300	1999	$50.9
767-300ER	2000	$38.4
767-200ER	1990	$10.1

AIRCRAFT DATA

	TYPES OF AIRCRAFT			
	A330-200	A330-300	767-200ER	767-300ER
# in Fleet	350	276	93	529
# of Operators	61	33	27	77
# on Order	210	113	0	28
Geographic Distribution				
Europe	113	48	14	137
Africa-Mid East	94	13	11	35
Asia-Pacific	99	171	9	102
North America	21	41	48	214
South America	23	3	11	41
Avg. Age of Fleet	5.2	6.7	18.3	13.4

★ ★ ★

22. Types of Journey Classes

REDEFINING FIRST CLASS

Imagine sleeping on a fully flat bed in your own private bedroom, 30,000 feet above the earth! Close the dual sliding doors to create your own private suite, offering unrivalled privacy and more personal space than one can imagine. It's not a dream; it's today's luxurious new First Class.

With only 8 seats in the cabin and a seat pitch of 90 inches you'll be travelling in utmost comfort. When it's time to unwind, slip on your Bose noise cancelling headphones and enjoy the latest in-flight entertainment on your 23-inch flat screen TV. You can relax through the journey by watching from over a number of movies, various business programmes and a number of short programmes. There are also various audio channels so you can listen to the music of your choice. Of course, it's all on demand so you control what you watch and when you watch it.

Want to work from your private bedroom? The airline provides you with a laptop power plug and adapters, so that you can be thoroughly prepared for your business by the time you arrive.

Your personal amenity kit boasts of EDT, comb, a razor and shaving cream, socks, mouthwash, toothbrush and moisturizer and a body lotion. Other articles that are provided for your comfort are lip balms, facial sprays, sleeper suits, eye masks and slippers. There's a private wardrobe, too. So you'll arrive in style no matter where your travels take you.

Come dinnertime, select from a tantalizing menu specially created to suit your palate. Personalize your five-course meal and choose what you want and when you want from the wide selection of world-class cuisine. Be spoilt for choice with two of the world's finest champagne, or appreciate the extensive selection of fine award-winning wines.

Explore the exclusive single malt library. Or try the airline's Cocktail for a change.

To further enhance the ambience, a phased mood-lighting system throughout the aircraft is often operational.

EXECUTIVE OR BUSINESS CLASS

Work while you fly or stretch out and relax in the most spacious seat in the sky.

Premiere class features a revolutionary lie-flat bed, surrounding you with a wall of privacy and personal space. The chairs are so arranged to provide easy access for all the passengers.

With only 30 seats in the cabin, all seats are aisle seats, designed to provide you utmost comfort. At a seat pitch of 49 inches, you can stretch out in luxury and settle down in the plush Premiere.

If you prefer to catch up with your work, there's a laptop power plug and adapters, so that you can wrap up your work in no time.

Prefer to give work a rest for a change? Treat yourself to well-deserved leisure time and enjoy from amongst 80 movies, various TV news programmes and short programmes on your huge 15.4-inch flat screen TV.

On board, you'll get an amenity kit which contains branded cologne, socks, a razor and shaving cream, mouthwash, toothbrush and a body lotion. Pamper yourself to the hilt.

Peruse the menu, whilst sipping Dom Perignon Champagne. Or if you're feeling peckish, help yourself to a snack from the dry bar. It's all part of the service.

ECONOMY CLASS

Reignite your enjoyment of flying and be inspired by today's spacious new Economy.

Some airlines have installed revolutionary seats designed to offer more space, reduce pressure on your body and give you added support, especially on long journeys. Simply recline your backrest and the seat bottom automatically moves into an ergonomically correct position.

Even the new headrest and unique footrest is designed to help you relax. So you can arrive at your destination more refreshed.

You may have a personal 10.6-inch touch screen TV that delivers the same on demand in-flight entertainment as enjoyed by the First Class and Premiere passengers. Create your own play list of over 200 songs or choose from a list of interactive games to keep even the most fanatical of gamers entertained.

Of course, there are plenty of games to keep the younger passengers entertained too.

★ ★ ★

23. Some Info for Passengers

HOTEL ACCOMMODATION POLICY FOR INTERNATIONAL PASSENGERS

Cancellation and Flight Delays

In the event of a flight being cancelled, the cancelled flight passengers are provided hotel accommodation provided their tickets are purchased from places other than the place of departure. Other passengers are given transport charges to their residence.

Passengers service voucher will be offered if the connecting time between the domestic and the international flight or vice-versa is more than 6 hours and within 24 hours.

No passenger service voucher will be provided in case the connecting flight is 24 hours after the passenger's arrival at the connecting point.

Hotel accommodation for international transit passengers will be available only at the Gateway points in India *i.e.*, Mumbai, Delhi, Kolkata and Chennai.

Hotel accommodation will be available for passengers travelling in First Class or Premiere.

This facility will be offered if the passengers hold bookings in the following classes:

- India - Europe - India and vice versa (Includes flights to London - Heathrow and Brussels): F, A, C and J class.
- India - North America and vice versa (Includes flights to USA and Canada)-India: F, A, C and J class.-India-South-East Asia and vice versa (Includes flights to Singapore, Bangkok, Kuala Lumpur, Katmandu and Colombo)-India: C class.

Passengers can avail themselves of this facility only if they hold confirmed onward bookings before their arrival at the transit point.

Tickets issued within 72 hours prior to departure will not be eligible for this facility.

Reservations for hotel accommodation must be done on the same PNR.

The airline is not liable for any loss, damage or expense incurred by the passengers because of the use of any extra services not mentioned above.

HOTEL ACCOMMODATION POLICY FOR DOMESTIC PASSENGERS

All benefits of transportation and accommodation are available for passengers travelling on full fare tickets only.

This facility is not available for passengers travelling on Check Fares.

In case of delays/cancellations which are communicated well in advance, passengers are requested to check the flight status before leaving for the airport.

Passengers travelling with tickets issued from station of departure will be provided with transport to the place of residence/hotel by airline and Rs. 1500 will be paid in the form of an MCO (Miscellaneous Charge Order). No hotel accommodation will be provided.

In the event of a flight diversion, passengers travelling on flights diverted to stations other than the station of departure would be provided with hotel accommodation, if available.

Transportation and accommodation facilities are not available for passengers travelling on discounted fare tickets (e.g. Check Fares).

E-TICKET COMPLIANCE

IATA (International Air Transport Association) has withdrawn all paper tickets stock from the BSPs (Billing and Settlement Plan). Thus, all BSP travel agents will not be able to issue neutral paper documents anymore, therefore paper ticket will only be issued by the airline for the Travel Agent in the case of the following non-eticket eligible situation.

Non-interline E-ticketing partners.

Interline-infant ticketing with interline e-ticketing partners which cannot support infant e-ticketing.

Stretcher / extra seat / cabin baggage / musical instruments.

Non e-ticket eligible code share flights of interline partners.

Non e-ticket eligible flights (future destinations) and non-air segment flights (bus services).

One fare pass.

It is advisable that all paper tickets are collected from airline counters at least 24 hours prior departure.

ELECTRONIC SYSTEM FOR TRAVEL AUTHORIZATION (ESTA)

Since August 1, 2008, the Electronic System for Travel Authorization (ESTA) has been introduced on a voluntary basis via Internet for citizens and eligible nationals of Visa Waiver Programme (VWP) countries to apply for advance authorization to travel to the United States under the VWP.

Visit USA strongly recommends to its members and to travel agents to encourage their clients to log on the ESTA system as from now in order to get them acquainted with this system which is mandatory from January 12, 2009.

One has to complete an on-line application. Travellers are encouraged to apply early. The web-based system will prompt one to answer basic biographical and eligibility questions typically requested on a paper I-94W form.

Applications may be submitted at any time prior to travel, however, DHS recommends that applications be submitted no less than 72 hours prior to travel. In most cases, you will receive a response within seconds:

1. *Authorization approved:* Travel authorized.
2. *Travel not authorized:* Traveller must obtain a non-immigrant visa at a U.S. Embassy or Consulate before travelling to the U.S.
3. *Authorization Pending:* Traveller will need to check the ESTA website for updates within 72 hours to receive a final response.

IMPORTANT NOTICE FOR ALL INDIAN PASSENGERS

A copy of the PAN Card duly attested by the passenger is mandatory when the sale of the air tickets for foreign travel exceeds Rs.25,000/- (per ticket) and the payment is made against CASH.

In the event that the passenger does not have a PAN Card and the sale of the ticket exceeds Rs.25,000/- (per ticket), a signed Declaration Form 60 will be required from the passenger. The Declaration Form 61 is only applicable to passengers who have agricultural income. The photocopy of the document as proof of address required in Form 60 and 61 must be duly signed by the passenger.

Please note that tickets will not be released by the cashier without the above documentation.

IDENTITY DOCUMENTS REQUIRED FOR INDIAN CITIZENS

Nepalese and Indian citizens must be in possession of any of the following documents while travelling by air between India and Nepal to establish their identity as Nepalese or Indian citizens.

(i) Valid national Passport.

(ii) Photo identity card issued by the Government of India/State Government/UT Administration in India to their employees or Election ID Card issued by the Election Commission of India.

(iii) Emergency certificate issued by Embassy of India, Kathmandu.

(iv) Identity certificate issued by Embassy of India, Kathmandu.

Persons in the age group of above 65 years and below 15 years are exempted from the requirement of the above-mentioned identity documents. However, they must have some documents with photograph to confirm their age and identity such as PAN card, driving license, CGHS card, ration card, etc.

SPECIAL INFORMATION

- For Gulf destinations (except Saudi Arabia), there may be visas arranged by sponsors, which are available at the destination. In the absence of the original visa, passengers must hold a photocopy of the valid visa.
- Passengers going to Saudi Arabia must have a valid Saudi visa, which will be affixed on the passport.
- "Visa on Arrival" should only be used to cases where immigration will issue a visa on arrival.
- All international flights to USA, originating from Mumbai and Delhi will undergo enhanced security checks. All the passengers are required to remove their footwear / shoes at the secondary security check located at terminal security points.
- For Australia and Africa, health card with valid inoculations is a must. The passenger should have completed the incubation period from the date of taking the inoculations; so that he is in the clear before he boards the flight. Otherwise, he becomes the responsibility of the airline, incase he is quarantined at destination, on medical grounds. Sometimes, airlines have to fly the passenger back on the return sector due to negligence at origin point.

INFANT/CHILD CARE

Child below 12 years can travel with an escort crew, at an additional charge, if requested for in advance. In that event, the crew only attends to his ward's needs, though sitting as a passenger in the cabin and dressed in uniform. Sometimes, if the young passenger just needs supervision alone that can be done by staff on duty on that flight, at no additional cost. The ground staff too hands over the UNM or YP to the crew working in that particular zone.

Duty-free shopping can be indulged in, on board. One can also seek guidance regarding customs regulations, so as to purchase only that quantity of alcohol; and cigarettes, as is allowed for that particular destiny.

For children below 12, a variety of comics, stuffed toys, colouring books with crayons, chocolates, etc. are kept on board to amuse the young ones. Playing card decks are available for adults, on request and can be given complimentarily.

Carriage of pets in cabin is allowed with captain's permission taken at the time of check in. Expectant mothers can travel till 32 weeks of their term.

For first and business class, services are so lavish that all airlines are going to the end of the world to provide personalized comfort and service to their guests. There are the much publicized flat beds, enclosing partitions with a personal bar, meals that are served at your convenience. One can even customize one's meal! Needless to mention, the most exclusive vintage wines and champagnes are given unlimitedly. These travellers can also use the lounge deck relax in and sprawl in exclusively, with attentive crew at their beck and call. It is indeed the last word in pampering.

An amenity kit containing slippers, a dressing robe, EDT, comb, razor and gel, toothbrush and mouthwash, moisturizer etc are presented to each traveller. In Y class, the seats are ergonomically designed and have a footrest and head rest, wide pitch in seats, on demand entertainment also.

Preflight services include welcome drink, offering newspapers and magazines, hot/cold towel or even a distribution of headsets or pillows and blankets.

★ ★ ★

24. The World Airlines

OPERATIONAL AIRLINES IN INDIA

Airlines	*IATA*	*Commenced Operations*	*Fleet Size*
Air India	AI	October 1932	127
Air-India Express	IX	April 2005	25
Air-India Regional	CD	September 2007	16
Blue Dart Aviation	BZ	May 1994	8
Club One Air		August 2005	1
Kingfisher Red	DN	August 2003	20
GoAir	G8	June 2004	8
IndiGo Airlines	6E	August 2006	25
Jet Airways	9W	May 1993	81
Jet Lite	S2	April 2007	18
Kingfisher Airlines	IT	May 2005	45
MDLR Airlines	9H	March 2007	3
Paramount Airways	17	October 2005	6
SpiceJet	SG	May 2005	19
Taj Air (formerly: Megapode Airlines) An Air Charter Service	—	1993	3

PREMIER INDIAN AIRLINES

Indian (Air India & Indian Airlines)

Air India is the national airline of India with a worldwide network of passengers and cargo services. National Aviation Company of India Ltd. was created in 2007 to facilitate Air India to merge with Indian Airlines. Then there is Air India Express and Air India Cargo too. The main base of operations is Chattrapati Shivaji International Airport in Mumbai and in Delhi, it is Indira Gandhi International Airport. Air India has code share agreements with 12 other international airlines but once it joins "The Star Alliance" formally, all these will cease automatically. It connects 130 destinations worldwide. Air India is now the 2nd largest airline in India in terms of passengers carried after Jet airways, and followed closely by Kingfisher Airlines. In domestic market share, it is 3rd after Jet and Kingfisher.

The average age of the fleet is 10.8 years as of April 2008, and operates Airbus A310, Boeing 747 and 777 as part of its fleet.

Air India Express planes have some unique tail art in all their 737-800 flights, to reflect a facet of its varied culture. The logo of the airline is a flying swan with Konark Chakra placed inside it. Air India is recalled fondly for its earlier mascot "The Maharajah" in royal livery, showcasing royalty and personalized service. In fact, the "Maharaja Lounge" is offered to first and executive class passengers, and offers renowned care and luxury.

Indian Airlines, AI merger flawed?

The parliamentary committee on public undertakings, in its report tabled on March 12, 2010, has recommended that the NACIL (the company managing unified carrier Air India) should be a holding company "under which two separate wings NACIL, Indian Airlines with its headquarters at Delhi, and NACIL, Air India with its headquarters at Mumbai," should function.

The committee recommended that each wing should be headed by a managing director who would report to the NACIL chairman.

The committee also expressed the need for "capital infusion into the ailing public airline to make the company credit worthy for its operational credit requirements" and said the utilisaiton of aircraft should be hiked from the current nine hours per day per aircraft to an average utilisation of 16 hours.

Kingfisher Airlines

The overall cancellation rate of scheduled domestic airlines for February, 2010 was 1.5 per cent, while the overall on-time performance of scheduled domestic airlines was recorded at 79.4 per cent.

It is based in Bangalore, India. It operates 218 flights daily with a network of 38 destinations. Its other bases are Chattrapati Shivaji International Airport, Rajiv Gandhi and Indira Gandhi International Airport. Through one of its holding companies, United Breweries Group has a 50% stake in low-cost carrier Kingfisher Red, formerly known as Air Deccan.

Kingfisher is one of the six airlines worldwide to have a 5-star rating from Sky trax and is the most admired brand in Asia-pacific region. In domestic operations, Kingfisher has 14.3% and Kingfisher Red (Air deccan) has 13.5% share. The chairman is Vijay Mallya and currently he has a code sharing allover with Jet airways. It has a fleet size of 78 aircraft, with 178 orders pending and flies to 68 destinations (including Red destinations). The company slogan is "Fly the Good Times" and has the new Bollywood heroine Deepika Padukone as its brand ambassador. It has the most modern fleet consisting of ATR'S, Airbuses, among them A-380 for ultra long-haul flights.

It plans to open a hub at Amsterdam, Schiphol airport to provide connectivity between India and Africa, Europe and N. America. It is also awaiting approval to connect all the major Indian cities with its European hub. It is also having a flying partnership with KLM and also Hilton Hotels worldwide for Guest Rewards programme.

According to the HT-MaRS Consumer Satisfaction Survey, Kingfisher is the airline of choice on parameters such as flying experience, check-in process, approach to customers, in-flight entertainment, airport baggage service and arrival services. It comes second to Jet Airways in flight boarding and is the joint leader with jet on cabin crew. There are attendants at hand to help with luggage and children when you arrive. Kingfisher's valets (porters and loaders) make a great difference for guests. Kingfisher does a little extra, which passengers like. It is also seen a glamourous airline and people do like that, too. Then, of course, it serves excellent on-board cuisine.

The smartly turned out air-hostesses add to the glamour quotient. Kingfisher also scores over other airlines on inflight entertainment-it offers some of the latest films. For Kingfisher is the best due to its competitive fares and hygienic washrooms. Their service attitude makes all the difference.

Jet Airways

Its base is at Mumbai. It is the country's 2nd largest international airline and largest domestic one, along with Jetlite. It operates 400 daily flights to 64 destinations. It has an international hub at Brussels too.

Airline	No. of Passengers* (in lakhs)
1. Jet Airways & Jet Lite	10.1
2. Kingfisher & Kingfisher Red	8.8
3. Air India (domestic)	6.6
4. Indigo	5.8
5. SpiceJet	4.7
7. Go Air	2.1
7. Paramount	0.62

* Passengers carried by domestic Airlines in Feb'10

In 2008, it was honoured as the world's best long-haul airline after Singpore Airlines and has won other awards as best overall airline, as well as for it's catering. It has Jetlite and Jet cargo as its subsidiaries. It has a fleet of 87 aircraft, with advance orders in addition. It flies to 85 destinations through code sharing. It uses the slogan "The joy of flying" as all its aircraft and literature. The founder chairman is Mr. Naresh Goyal and an alliance is forged with Mr. Mallya of Kingfisher to include code sharing on both domestic and international flights to reduce expenses, joint fuel management, common ground handling etc. Earlier, Jet Airways bought over Air Sahara and are now called Jetlite, as a low cost carrier.

Its fleet has ATR'S, Airbus and a range of Boeings and its average age is 4-5 years in 2009.

WORLD'S MAJOR AIRLINES

Airlines	IATA Designator	Hub	Airlines	IATA Designator	Hub
Aeroflot	S4	Moscow	Japan Airlines	JL	Narita–Tokyo
Aeroméxico	AM	Mexico City	KLM Royal Dutch	KL	Amsterdam
Air Canada	AC	Montreal, Toronto	Korean Air	KE	Incheon–Seoul
Air China	CA	Beijing–China	Kuwait Airways	KU	Kuwait
Air France	AF	Paris–Charles de Gaulle	LOT Polish Airlines	LO	Kraków, Warsaw
Air India	AI, IC	Mumbai, Frankfurt	Lufthansa	LH	Düsseldorf, Frankfurt, Munich, Cancun
Air Jamaica	JM	Montego Bay	Mahan Air	W5	Iran
Air Mauritius	MK	Mauritius	Malaysia Airlines	MH	Kuala Lumpur
Alaska Airlines	AS	Anchorage	Mexicana	MX	Mexico City
Alitalia	AZ	Fiumicino–Rome	Oman Air	WY	Oman
All Nippon Airways	NH	Narita–Tokyo	Pakistan International Airlines	PK	Barcelona, Islamabad, Karachi, Lahore
American Airlines	AA	Miami, New York and others	Qantas Airways	QF	Sydney–Australia
Asiana Airlines	OZ	Incheon–Seoul	Qatar Airways	QR	Doha
Austrian Airlines	OS	Vienna	Royal Jordanian	RJ	Jordan
Biman Airlines	BG	Dhaka–Bangladesh	Singapore Airlines	SQ	Singapore
British Airways	BA	Heathrow–London	Srilankan Airlines	UL	Colombo
Cathay Pacific	CX	Hong Kong	Swiss International Air lines	LX	Zürich
China Airlines	CI	China	Thai Airways	TG	Bangkok–Thailand
Continental Airlines	CO	Houston-Intercontinental, Newark	United Airlines	UA	Cancun, Charlotte and others
Delta Air Lines	DL	Atlanta, Detroit, Memphis	US Airways	US	Charlotte, Philadelphia, Phoenix
Emirates Airlines	EK	Dubai	Virgin Atlantic Airways	VS	London
Etihad Airways	EY	Abu Dhabi			
Finn Air	AY	Finland			
Garuda	GA	Indonesia			
Gulf Air	GF	Bahrain			
Iberia	IB	Madrid–Spain			

25. Airlines Logos

LOGOS OF FAMOUS NATIONAL AND INTERNATIONAL AIRLINES

1. BRITISH AIRWAYS

2. CATHAY PACIFIC

3. 

4. Continental Airlines

5. DELTA

6. DRAGONAIR

7. АЭРОФЛОТ Российские авиалинии

8. AEROMEXICO

9.

10.

11.

12.

13.

14.

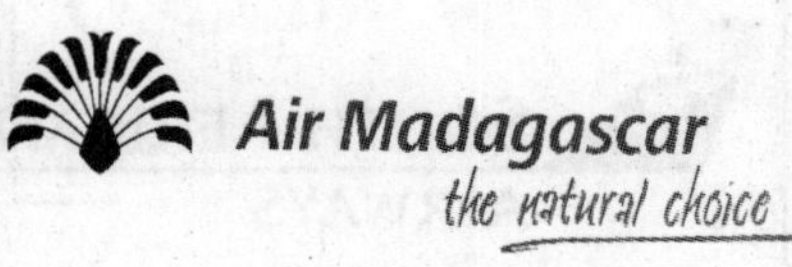

15.

16.

17.

18.

19.

20.

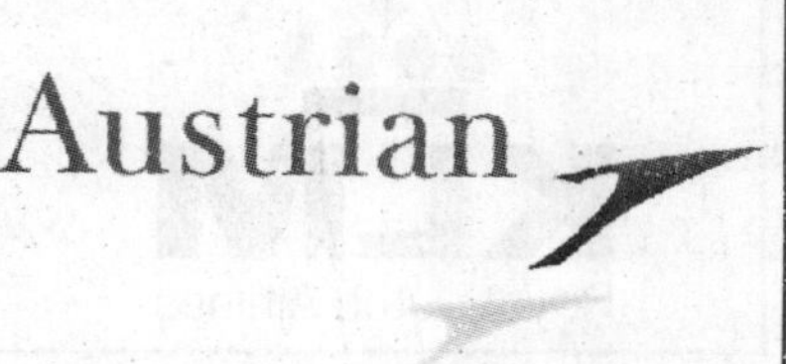

21.

22.

23.

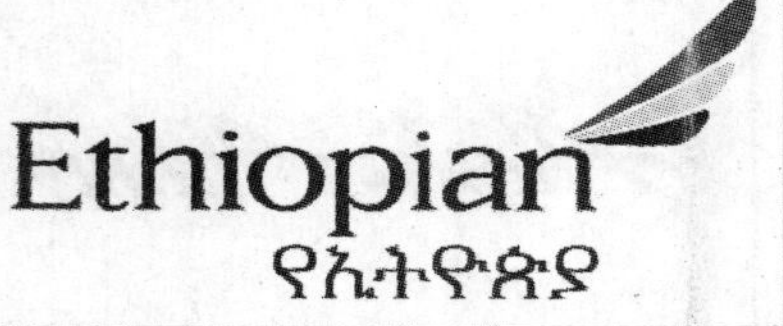

24.

25.

26.

27.

KOREAN AIR

28.

29.

30.

31.

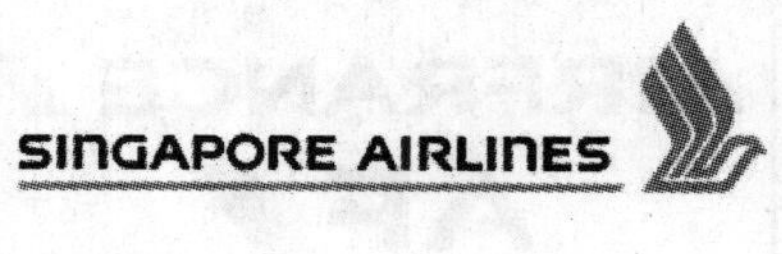

32.

33.

34.

35.

36.

37.

38.

★ ★ ★

26. Airports of The World

MAJOR WORLD AIRPORTS

Country	*City*	*Code*	*Airport Name*
Albania	Tirana	TIA	Rinas Airport
Anguilla	Anguilla Island	AXA	Wallblake Airport
Antigua and Barbuda	Saint Johns	ANU	VC Bird International Airport
Argentina	Buenos Aires	EZE	Ministro Pistarini International Airport
Aruba	Aruba Island	AUA	Queen Beatrix International Airport
Australia	Adelaide	ADL	Adelaide International Airport
Australia	Brisbane	BNE	Brisbane International Airport
Australia	Cairns	CNS	Cairns International Airport
Australia	Canberra	CBR	Canberra Airport
Australia	Coolangatta	OOL	Gold Coast Airport
Australia	Darwin	DRW	Darwin International Airport
Australia	Hobart	HBA	Hobart Airport
Australia	Launceston	LST	Launceston Airport
Australia	Melbourne	MEL	Melbourne International Airport
Australia	Perth	PER	Perth International Airport
Australia	Sydney	SYD	Kingsford Smith International Airport
Austria	Innsbruck	INN	Innsbruck Airport
Austria	Vienna	VIE	Vienna International Airport
Azerbaijan	Baku	BAK	Baku Airport
Bahamas	Abaco Island	MHH	Marsh Harbour Airport
Bahamas	Abaco Island	TCB	Treasure Cay Airport
Bahamas	Andros Island	ASD	Andros Town International Airport

Country	City	Code	Airport Name
Bahamas	Bimini	BIM	Bimini Island International Airport
Bahamas	Cat Island	TBI	New Bight Airport
Bahamas	Eleuthera Island	ELH	North Eleuthera Airport
Bahamas	Freeport	FPO	Freeport International Airport
Bahamas	Great Exuma Island	GGT	Exuma International Airport
Bahamas	Nassau	NAS	Nassau International Airport
Bahrain	Bahrain	BAH	Bahrain International Airport
Bangladesh	Dhaka	DAC	Zia International Airport
Barbados	Bridgetown	BGI	Grantley Adams International Airport
Belgium	Brussels	BRU	Brussels International Airport
Belgium	Brussels	CRL	Charleroi Airport
Belize	Belize City	BZE	Phillip S W Goldson Airport
Benin	Cotonou	COO	Cadjehoun Airport
Bermuda	Bermuda Island	BDA	Bermuda International Airport
Bolivia	La Paz	LPB	El Alto International Airport
Bolivia	Santa Cruz	VVI	Viru Viru International Airport
Brazil	Brasilia	BSB	Kubitschek International Airport
Brazil	Campo Grande	CGR	Campo Grande International Airport
Brazil	Cuiaba	CGB	Marechal Rondon International Airport
Brazil	Curitiba	CWB	Afonso Pena International Airport
Brazil	Florianopolis	FLN	Hercillio Luz International Airport
Brazil	Fortaleza	FOR	Pinto Martins International Airport
Brazil	Iguassa Falls	IGU	Iguassa Falls Airport
Brazil	Londrina	LDB	Londrina Airport
Brazil	Manaus	MAO	Eduardo Gomes International Airport
Brazil	Navegantes	NVT	Navegantes-Itajai Airport
Brazil	Porto Alegre	POA	Salgado Filho International Airport
Brazil	Recife	REC	Guararapes International Airport
Brazil	Rio de Janeiro	GIG	Rio de Janeiro International Airport
Brazil	Salvador	SSA	Salvador International Airport
Brazil	Sao Paulo	CGH	Congonhas International Airport
Brazil	Sao Paulo	GRU	Guarulhos International Airport

Country	City	Code	Airport Name
Burkina Faso	Ouagadougou	OUA	Ouagadougou Airport
Cameroon	Douala	DLA	Douala Airport
Cameroon	Yaounde	NSI	Nsimalen Airport
Canada	Calgary	YYC	Calgary International Airport
Canada	Edmonton	YEG	Edmonton International Airport
Canada	Fredericton	YFC	Greater Fredericton Airport
Canada	Halifax	YHZ	Halifax International Airport
Canada	Kelowna	YLW	City of Kelowna Airport
Canada	London	YXU	London Airport
Canada	Moncton	YQM	Moncton International Airport
Canada	Montreal	YMX	Mirabel International Airport
Canada	Montreal	YUL	Montreal Dorval Airport
Canada	Ottawa	YOW	Ottawa International Airport
Canada	Quebec City	YQB	Jean Lesage International Airport
Canada	Regina	YQR	Regina International Airport
Canada	Saint John's	YYT	St John's International Airport
Canada	Saskatoon	YXE	Saskatoon International Airport
Canada	Sydney	YQY	Sydney Airport
Canada	Thunder Bay	YQT	Thunder Bay International Airport
Canada	Toronto	YYZ	Lester B Pearson International Airport
Canada	Vancouver	YVR	Vancouver International Airport
Canada	Victoria	YYJ	Victoria International Airport
Canada	Winnipeg	YWG	Winnipeg International Airport
Cape Verde	Sal	SID	Amilcar Cabral International Airport
Cayman Islands	Grand Cayman	GCM	Owen Roberts International Airport
Chad	N'Djamena	NDJ	N'Djamena Airport
Chile	Antofagasta	ANF	Cerro Moreno International Airport
Chile	Concepcion	CCP	Carriel Sur International Airport
Chile	Iquique	IQQ	Diego Aracena International Airport
Chile	Mataveri	IPC	Easter Island Airport
Chile	Puerto Montt	PMC	El Tepual International Airport
Chile	Punta Arenas	PUQ	Punta Arenas International Airport

Country	City	Code	Airport Name
Chile	Santiago	SCL	Benitez International Airport
China	Beijing	PEK	Beijing Capital International Airport
China	Chengdu	CTU	Shuangliu Airport
China	Chongqing	CKG	Jiangbei Airport
China	Fuzhou	FOC	Changle Airport
China	Guangzhou	CAN	Baiyun Airport
China	Hong Kong	HKG	Hong Kong International Airport
China	Shanghai	PVG	Pudong Airport
China	Shanghai	SHA	Hongqiao International Airport
China	Shenyang	SHE	Taoxian Airport
China	Shenzhen	SZX	Huangtian Airport
China	Xi'an	XIY	Xianyang Airport
Colombia	Barranquilla	BAQ	Ernesto Cortissoz Airport
Colombia	Bogota	BOG	Eldorado International Airport
Colombia	Cali	CLO	Aragon International Airport
Colombia	Cartagena	CTG	Rafael Nunez Airport
Colombia	Medellin	MDE	Jose Maria Cordova International Airport
Colombia	Pereira	PEI	Matecana International Airport
Congo	Brazzaville	BZV	Maya-Maya Airport
Cook Islands	Rarotonga Island	RAR	Rarotonga International Airport
Costa Rica	Liberia	LIR	Daniel Oduber Quiros International Airport
Costa Rica	San Jose	SJO	Juan Santa Maria International Airport
Croatia	Split	SPU	Kastela Airport
Croatia	Zagreb	ZAG	Pleso Airport
Cuba	Havana	HAV	Jose Marti International Airport
Cyprus	Larnaca	LCA	Larnaca International Airport
Czech Republic	Ostrava	OSR	Mosnov Airport
Czech Republic	Prague	PRG	Ruzyne International Airport
Denmark	Aalborg	AAL	Aalborg Airport
Denmark	Aarhus	AAR	Aarhus Airport
Denmark	Billund	BLL	Billund Airport
Denmark	Copenhagen	CPH	Kastrup International Airport

Country	*City*	*Code*	*Airport Name*
Dominica	Roseau	DOM	Melville Hall Airport
Dominican Republic	La Romana	LRM	La Romana International Airport
Dominican Republic	Puerto Plata	POP	La Union International Airport
Dominican Republic	Punta Cana	PUJ	Punta Cana International Airport
Dominican Republic	Santiago City	STI	Cibao International Airport
Dominican Republic	Santo Domingo	SDQ	Las Americas International Airport
Ecuador	Guayaquil	GYE	Simon Bolivar International Airport
Ecuador	Quito	UIO	Mariscal Sucre International Airport
Egypt	Alexandria	HBE	Borg El Arab International Airport
Egypt	Cairo	CAI	Cairo International Airport
El Salvador	San Salvador	SAL	Comalapa International Airport
Equatorial Guinea	Malabo	SSG	Malabo Airport
Estonia	Talinn	TLL	Ulemiste Airport
Ethiopia	Addis Ababa	ADD	Bole International Airport
Fiji	Nadi	NAN	Nadi International Airport
Finland	Helsinki	HEL	Vantaa International Airport
France	Basle-Mulhouse	MLH	Basle-Mulhouse Airport
France	Biarritz	BIQ	Bayonne-Anglet Airport
France	Bordeaux	BOD	Merignac Airport
France	Brest	BES	Guipavas Airport
France	Clermont-Ferrand	CFE	Aulnat Airport
France	Grenoble	GNB	St Geoirs Airport
France	Limoges	LIG	Bellegarde Airport
France	Lyon	LYS	Satolas Airport
France	Marseille/Provence	MRS	Marseille/Provence Airport
France	Montpellier	MPL	Montpellier Airport
France	Nantes	NTE	Nantes Airport
France	Nice	NCE	Cote d'Azur International Airport
France	Paris	CDG	Charles De Gaulle International Airport
France	Paris	LBG	Le Bourget Airport
France	Paris	ORY	Orly Airport
France	Rennes	RNS	St Jacques Airport

Country	City	Code	Airport Name
France	Strasbourg	SXB	Entzheim Airport
France	Toulouse	TLS	Blagnac Airport
French Polynesia	Tahiti Island	PPT	Papeete Faaa Airport
Gabon	Libreville	LBV	Leon M'ba
Gambia	Banjul	BJL	Banjul International Airport
Germany	Berlin	SXF	Schonefeld Airport
Germany	Berlin	TXL	Tegel Airport
Germany	Bremen	BRE	Bremen Airport
Germany	Cologne-Bonn	CGN	Cologne-Bonn Airport
Germany	Duesseldorf	DUS	Duesseldorf International Airport
Germany	Frankfurt	FRA	Frankfurt International Airport
Germany	Hamburg	HAM	Hamburg Airport
Germany	Hannover	HAJ	Hannover Airport
Germany	Munich	MUC	Franz Josef Strauss International Airport
Germany	Nuremberg	NUE	Nuremberg Airport
Germany	Stuttgart	STR	Echterdingen International Airport
Ghana	Accra	ACC	Kotoka International Airport
Greece	Athens	ATH	Athens International Airport
Grenada	Saint Georges	GND	Point Salines International Airport
Guadeloupe	Point-A-Pitre	PTP	Le Raizet International Airport
Guam	Guam	GUM	Guam International Airport
Guatemala	Flores	FRS	Tikal International Airport
Guatemala	Guatemala City	GUA	La Aurora International Airport
Guinea	Conakry	CKY	Gbessia
Guyana	Georgetown	GEO	Cheddi Jagan International Airport
Haiti	Port-au-Prince	PAP	Port-au-Prince International Airport
Honduras	Roatan	RTB	Roatan Island Airport
Honduras	San Pedro Sula	SAP	La Mesa International Airport
Honduras	Tegucigalpa	TGU	Toncontin International Airport
Hungary	Budapest	BUD	Ferihegy Airport
Iceland	Keflavik	KEF	Keflavik International Airport
Indonesia	Den Pasar	DPS	Bali International Airport

Country	City	Code	Airport Name
Indonesia	Jakarta	CGK	Soekarno-Hatta International Airport
Indonesia	Surabaya	SUB	Juanda Airport
Iran	Tehran	THR	Mehrabad International Airport
Ireland	Dublin	DUB	Dublin International Airport
Ireland	Shannon	SNN	Shannon International Airport
Israel	Tel Aviv	TLV	Ben Gurion International Airport
Italy	Ancona	AOI	Falconara Airport
Italy	Bari	BRI	Palese Macchie Airport
Italy	Bologna	BLQ	Borgo Panigale Airport
Italy	Brindisi	BDS	Brindisi P Casale Airport
Italy	Catania	CTA	Fontanarossa Airport
Italy	Florence	FLR	Peretola Airport
Italy	Genoa	GOA	Sestri Airport
Italy	Lamezia	SUF	Terme Airport
Italy	Milan	LIN	Linate Airport
Italy	Milan	MXP	Malpensa International Airport
Italy	Naples	NAP	Capodichino Airport
Italy	Palermo	PMO	Punta Raisi Airport
Italy	Pisa	PSA	San Giusto Airport
Italy	Reggio Calabria	REG	Reggio Calabria Airport
Italy	Rome	CIA	Ciampino Airport
Italy	Rome	FCO	Fiumicino Airport
Italy	Torino	TRN	Caselle Airport
Italy	Trieste	TRS	Ronchi Dei Legionari Airport
Italy	Venice	VCE	Tessera Airport
Ivory Coast	Abidjan	ABJ	Felix Houphouet-Boigny Airport
Jamaica	Kingston	KIN	Norman Manley International Airport
Jamaica	Montego Bay	MBJ	Sangster International Airport
Japan	Akita	AXT	Akita Airport
Japan	Aomori	AOJ	Aomori Airport
Japan	Asahikawa	AKJ	Asahikawa Airport
Japan	Fukuoka	FUK	Fukuoka Airport

Country	City	Code	Airport Name
Japan	Fukushima	FKS	Fukushima Airport
Japan	Hakodate	HKD	Hakodate Airport
Japan	Hiroshima	HIJ	Hiroshima Airport
Japan	Kagoshima	KOJ	Kagoshima Airport
Japan	Nagasaki	NGS	Nagasaki Airport
Japan	Nagoya	NGO	Nagoya Airport
Japan	Niigata	KIJ	Niigata Airport
Japan	Oita	OIT	Oita Airport
Japan	Okayama	OKJ	Okayama Airport
Japan	Okinawa Island	DNA	Okinawa Kadena Airport
Japan	Osaka	ITM	Osaka International Airport
Japan	Osaka	KIX	Kansai International Airport
Japan	Sapporo	CTS	New Chitose Airport
Japan	Sendai	SDJ	Sendai Airport
Japan	Tokyo	HND	Tokyo International Airport
Japan	Tokyo	NRT	Narita International Airport
Japan	Toyama	TOY	Toyama Airport
Jordan	Amman	ADJ	Marka International Airport
Jordan	Amman	AMM	Queen Alia International Airport
Kazahkstan	Almaty	ALA	Almaty Airport
Kenya	Nairobi	NBO	Jomo Kenyatta Airport
Kuwait	Kuwait City	KWI	Kuwait International Airport
Laos	Vientiane	VTE	Wattay International Airport
Latvia	Riga	RIX	Riga International Airport
Lebanon	Beirut	BEY	Beirut International Airport
Luxembourg	Luxembourg	LUX	Luxembourg Airport
Malaysia	Kuala Lumpur	KUL	Kuala Lumpur International Airport
Malaysia	Penang Island	PEN	Penang International Airport
Mali	Bamako	BKO	Senou International Airport
Marshall Islands	Kwajalein Atoll	KWA	Kwajalein International Airport
Marshall Islands	Majuro Atoll	MAJ	Marshall Islands International Airport
Mauritania	Nouakchott	NKC	Nouakchott Airport

Country	City	Code	Airport Name
Mexico	Acapulco	ACA	Juan N Alvarez International Airport
Mexico	Aguascalientes	AGU	Jesus Teran International Airport
Mexico	Bahia De Huatulco	HUX	Huatulc International Airport
Mexico	Cabo San Lucas	SJD	Los Cab International Airport
Mexico	Cancun	CUN	Cancun ernational Airport
Mexico	Chetumal	CTM	Chetumal International Airport
Mexico	Chihuahua	CUU	General Fierro Villalobos Airport
Mexico	iudad Del Carmen	CME	Ciudad del Carmen Airport
Mexico	iudad Juarez	CJS	Gonzalez International Airport
Mexico	Cozume!	CZM	Cozumel International Airport
Mexico	Culiacan	CUL	Culiacan International Airport
Mexico	Durango	DGO	Durango Airport
Mexico	Guadalajara	GDL	Don Miguel Hidalgo International Airport
Mexico	Guerrero Negro	GUB	Guerrero Negro Airport
Mexico	Hermosillo	HMO	Garcia Airport
Mexico	La Paz	LAP	Manuel de Leon Airport
Mexico	Leon	BJX	De Guanajuato International Airport
Mexico	Loreto	LTO	Loreto International Airport
Mexico	Los Mochis	LMM	Valle Del Fuerte International Airport
Mexico	Manzanillo	ZLO	Playa De Oro International Airport
Mexico	Mazatlan	MZT	Mazatlan International Airport
Mexico	Merida	MID	Licenciado Manuel International Airport
Mexico	Mexicali	MXL	Toboada International Airport
Mexico	Mexico City	MEX	Benito Juarez International Airport
Mexico	Minatitlan	MTT	Minitatlan Airport
Mexico	Monclova	LOV	Monclova International Airport
Mexico	Monterrey	MTY	Monterrey International Airport
Mexico	Monterrey	NTR	Del Norte International Airport
Mexico	Morelia	MLM	Mujica International Airport
Mexico	Oaxaca	OAX	Xoxocotlan International Airport
Mexico	Puebla	PBC	Hermanos Serdan International Airport
Mexico	Puerto Escondido	PXM	Puerto Escondido Airport

Country	City	Code	Airport Name
Mexico	Puerto Vallarta	PVR	Lic Gustavo Diaz Ordaz International Air
Mexico	Queretaro	QRO	Ingeniero International Airport
Mexico	Saltillo	SLW	Plan De Guadalupe International Airport
Mexico	San Luis Potosi	SLP	Ponciano Arriaga International Airport
Mexico	Tampico	TAM	Tampico Airport
Mexico	Tapachula	TAP	Tapachula International Airport
Mexico	Tijuana	TIJ	Rodriguez International Airport
Mexico	Toluca	TLC	Toluca International Airport
Mexico	Torreon	TRC	Torreon International Airport
Mexico	Tuxtla Gutierrez	TGZ	Francisco Sarabia Airport
Mexico	Veracruz	VER	Veracruz International Airport
Mexico	Villahermosa	VSA	Carlos Rovirosa International Airport
Mexico	Zacatecas	ZCL	Ruiz International Airport
Mexico	Zihuatanejo	ZIH	Ixtapa-Zihuatanejo International Airport
Micronesia	Babelthuap Island	ROR	Babelthuap/Koror Airport
Micronesia	Kosrae	KSA	Kosrae Island Airport
Micronesia	Pohnpei Island	PNI	Pohnpei International Airport
Micronesia	Truk	TKK	Truk Airport
Micronesia	Yap Island	YAP	Yap International Airport
Morocco	Agadir	AGA	Al-Massira Airport
Morocco	Casablanca	CMN	Mohammed V International Airport
Morocco	Marrakech	RAK	Menara Airport
Morocco	Rabat	RBA	Sale Airport
Morocco	Tangier	TNG	Ibn Batouta Airport
Namibia	Windhoek	WDH	Hosea Kutako International Airport
Netherlands	Amsterdam	AMS	Schipol Airport
Netherlands	Maastricht	MST	Maastricht-Aachen Airport
Netherlands Antilles	Bonaire Island	BON	Flamingo Airport
Netherlands Antilles	Curacao Island	CUR	Hato International Airport
Netherlands Antilles	Saint Maarten	SXM	Princess Juliana International Airport
New Zealand	Auckland	AKL	Auckland International Airport
New Zealand	Christchurch	CHC	Christchurch International Airport

Country	City	Code	Airport Name
New Zealand	Dunedin	DUD	Dunedin Airport
New Zealand	Queenstown	ZQN	Queenstown Airport
New Zealand	Wellington	WLG	Wellington International Airport
Nicaragua	Managua	MGA	Managua International Airport
Niger	Niamey	NIM	Diori Hamani Airport
Nigeria	Abuja	ABV	Nnamdi Azikiwe Airport
Nigeria	Kano	KAN	Mallam Aminu Kano Airport
Nigeria	Lagos	LOS	Lagos International Airport
Nigeria	Port Harcourt	PHC	Port Harcourt Airport
Northern Marianas	Rota Island	ROP	Rota Island International Airport
Northern Marianas	Saipan Island	SPN	Saipan International Airport
Norway	Bergen	BGO	Flesland Airport
Norway	Oslo	OSL	Oslo Airport, Gardermoen
Norway	Stavanger	SVG	Sola Airport
Norway	Torp	TRF	Sandefjord Airport
Norway	Trondheim	TRD	Trondheim Airport
Oman	Muscat	MCT	Seeb International Airport
Pakistan	Islamabad	ISB	Islamabad International Airport
Pakistan	Karachi	KHI	Quaid-E-Azam International Airport
Pakistan	Lahore	LHE	Lahore International Airport
Panama	Panama City	PFN	Panama City Airport
Panama	Panama City	PTY	Tocumen International Airport
Peru	Lima	LIM	Jorge Chavez International Airport
Philippines	Manila	MNL	Ninoy Aquino International Airport
Poland	Krakow	KRK	John Paul II Balice International Airport
Poland	Warsaw	WAW	Okecie International Airport
Portugal	Lisbon	LIS	Lisbon International Airport
Portugal	Oporto	OPO	Francisco Sa Carneiro Airport
Puerto Rico	Aguadilla	BQN	Rafael Hernandez Airport
Puerto Rico	Mayaguez	MAZ	Eugenio Maria De Hostos Airport
Puerto Rico	Ponce	PSE	Mercedita Airport
Puerto Rico	San Juan	SJU	Luiz Munoz Marin International Airport

Country	City	Code	Airport Name
Puerto Rico	Vieques	VQS	Antonio Rivera Rodriguez Airport
Qatar	Doha	DOH	Doha International Airport
Romania	Bucharest	OTP	Otopeni International Airport
Romania	Satu Mare	SUJ	Satu Mare International Airport
Romania	Timisoara	TSR	Timisoara Airport
Russia	Moscow	DME	Domodedovo Airport
Russia	Moscow	SVO	Sheremetyevo International Airport
Russia	Saint Petersburg	LED	Pulkovo International Airport
Saint Kitts and Nevis	Nevis Island	NEV	Newcastle Airport
Saint Kitts and Nevis	St Kitts Island	SKB	Robert Bradshaw International Airport
Saint Lucia	Castries	SLU	Vigie Airport
Saint Lucia	Saint Lucia	UVF	Hewanorra International Airport
Saint Vincent	Canouan Island	CIW	Canouan Island Airport
Saudi Arabia	Dammam	DMM	King Fahad International Airport
Saudi Arabia	Jeddah	JED	King Abdulaziz International Airport
Saudi Arabia	Riyadh	RUH	King Khaled International Airport
Senegal	Dakar	DKR	Dakar - Yoff International Airport
Serbia	Belgrade	BEG	Belgrade Airport
Singapore	Singapore	SIN	Changi International Airport
Slovakia	Bratislava	BTS	M R Stefanik Airport
Slovakia	Kosice	KSC	Kosice Airport
South Africa	Capetown	CPT	Capetown International Airport
South Africa	Durban	DUR	Durban International Airport
South Africa	East London	ELS	East London Airport
South Africa	George	GRJ	George Airport
South Africa	Johannesburg	JNB	Johannesburg International Airport
South Africa	Port Elizabeth	PLZ	Port Elizabeth Airport
South Korea	Pusan	PUS	Kimhae International Airport
South Korea	Seoul	GMP	Gimpo Airport
South Korea	Seoul	ICN	Incheon International Airport
Spain	Alicante	ALC	Alicante
Spain	Barcelona	BCN	Barcelona Airport

Country	City	Code	Airport Name
Spain	Bilbao	BIO	Bilbao Airport
Spain	La Palma	SPC	La Palma Airport
Spain	Madrid	MAD	Barajas International Airport
Spain	Madrid	TOJ	Torrejon Airport
Spain	Malaga	AGP	Malaga International Airport
Spain	Palma De Mallorca	PMI	Palma De Mallorca Airport
Spain	Tenerife-North	TFN	Los Rodeos Airport
Sweden	Goteborg	GOT	Landvetter Airport
Sweden	Stockholm	ARN	Arlanda International Airport
Switzerland	Basel	BSL	Basel International Airport
Switzerland	Geneva	GVA	Cointrin International Airport
Switzerland	Zurich	ZRH	Zurich International Airport
Syria	Aleppo	ALP	Aleppo International Airport
Syria	Damascus	DAM	Damascus International Airport
Taiwan	Kaohsiung	KHH	Kaohsiung International Airport
Taiwan	Taipei	TPE	Chiang Kai-Shek International Airport
Tanzania	Dar-Es-Salaam	DAR	Dar-Es-Salaam International Airport
Tanzania	Kilimanjaro	JRO	Kilimanjaro International Airport
Thailand	Bangkok	BKK	Don Muang International Airport
Togo	Lome	LFW	Tokoin Airport
Trinidad and Tobago	Port Of Spain	POS	Piarco International Airport
Tunisia	Tunis	TUN	Carthage Airport
Turkey	Istanbul	IST	Ataturk International Airport
Turks and Caicos	Providenciales	PLS	Providenciales International Airport
Uganda	Entebbe	EBB	Entebbe International Airport
UK Virgin Islands	Beef Island	EIS	Beef Island International Airport
Ukraine	Kiev	IEV	Zhulyany International Airport
Ukraine	Kiev	KBP	Borispol Airport
United Arab Emirates	Abu Dhabi	AUH	Abu Dhabi International Airport
United Arab Emirates	Dubai	DXB	Dubai International Airport
United Kingdom	Aberdeen	ABZ	Dyce Airport
United Kingdom	Belfast	BFS	Belfast International Airport

Country	City	Code	Airport Name
United Kingdom	Belfast	BHD	Belfast City Airport
United Kingdom	Birmingham	BHX	Birmingham International Airport
United Kingdom	Bristol	BRS	Bristol Airport
United Kingdom	Cardiff	CWL	Cardiff Airport
United Kingdom	Edinburgh	EDI	Edinburgh Airport
United Kingdom	Glasgow	GLA	Glasgow International Airport
United Kingdom	Guernsey	GCI	Guernsey Airport
United Kingdom	Humberside	HUY	Humberside Airport
United Kingdom	Inverness	INV	Inverness Airport
United Kingdom	Jersey	JER	Jersey Airport
United Kingdom	Leeds Bradford	LBA	Leeds Bradford Airport
United Kingdom	London	LCY	London City Airport
United Kingdom	London	LGW	London Gatwick Airport
United Kingdom	London	LHR	London Heathrow Airport
United Kingdom	London	STN	Stansted Airport
United Kingdom	Manchester	MAN	Manchester International Airport
United Kingdom	Newcastle	NCL	Newcastle Airport
United Kingdom	Norwich	NWI	Norwich Airport
United Kingdom	Southampton	SOU	Southampton International Airport
United Kingdom	Teesside	MME	Durham Tees Valley Airport
Uruguay	Montevideo	MVD	Carrasco International Airport
US Virgin Islands	Saint Croix	STX	Henry E Rohlsen Airport
US Virgin Islands	Saint Thomas	STT	Cyril E King International Airport
Uzbekistan	Tashkent	TAS	Vostochny International Airport
Venezuela	Caracas	CCS	Simon Bolivar International Airport
Venezuela	Maracaibo	MAR	La Chinita International Airport
Vietnam	Hanoi	HAN	Noibai International Airport
Vietnam	Ho Chi Minh City	SGN	Tansonnhat Airport
Western Samoa	Apia	APW	Faleolo International Airport
Zambia	Lusaka	LUN	Lusaka International Airport

MAJOR INDIAN AIRPORTS

City	*Code*	*Airport Name*
A & N ISLANDS (UNION TERRITORY)		
Port Blair	IXZ	Vir Savarkar Airport (Port Blair Airport)
ANDHRA PRADESH		
Kadapa (Cuddapah)	CDP	Cuddapah Airport
Hyderabad (International)	HYD	Hyderabad International Airport (Rajiv Gandhi International Airport)
Puttaparthi	BEK	Sri Sathya Sai Airport
Rajahmundry	RJA	Rajahmundry Airport
Tirumala - Tirupati (Tirupathi)	TIR	Tirupati Airport
Vijayawada (Vijaywada)	VGA	Vijayawada Airport (Vijaywada Airport)
Visakhapatnam (Vishakhapatnam)	VTZ	Visakhapatnam Airport (Vizag Airport)
Warangal (Warrangal)	WGC	Warangal Airport
ARUNACHAL PRADESH		
Along	IXV	Along Airport
Daporijo (Daporizo)	DAE	Daporijo Airport
Pasighat (Passighat)	IXT	Pasighat Airport
Tezu	TEI	Tezu Airport
Ziro	ZER	Zero Airport
ASSAM		
Dibrugarh	DIB	Dibrugarh Airport
Guwahati (International)	GAU	Lokpriya Gopinath Bordoloi International Airport
Jorhat	JRH	Jorhat Airport (Rowriah Airport)
North Lakhimpur	IXI	Lilabari Airport (North Lakhimpur Airport)
Silchar	IXS	Silchar Airport (Kumbhirgram Airport)
Tezpur	TEZ	Tezpur Airport (Tezpur Air Force Base)
BIHAR		
Gaya	GAY	Gaya Airport
Muzzafarpur	MZU	Muzzafarpur Airport
Patna	PAT	Lok Nayak Jayaprakash Airport (Patna Airport)
Purnia (Purnea)	PUI	Purnea Airport

City	Code	Airport Name
CHANDIGARH (UNION TERRITORY)		
Chandigarh	IXC	Chandigarh Airport
CHHATTISGARH		
Bilaspur	PAB	Bilaspur Airport
Jagdalpur	JGB	Jagdalpur Airport
Raipur	RPR	Raipur Airport
DAMAN AND DIU (UNION TERRITORY)		
Daman	NMB	Daman Airport
Diu	DIU	Diu Airport
DELHI (NATIONAL CAPITAL TERRITORY)		
New Delhi (International)	DEL	Indira Gandhi International Airport
New Delhi		Safdarjung Airport
GOA		
Dabolim / Vasco da Gama (International)	GOI	Dabolim Airport (Goa Airport)
GUJARAT		
Ahmedabad (International)	AMD	Sardar Vallabhbhai Patel International Airport
Bhavnagar	BHU	Bhavnagar Airport
Bhuj	BHJ	Bhuj Airport
Gandhidham / Kandla	IXY	Kandla Airport (Gandhidham Airport)
Jamnagar	JGA	Jamnagar Airport
Keshod	IXK	Junagadh Airport
Porbandar	PBD	Porbandar Airport
Rajkot	RAJ	Rajkot Airport
Surendranagar	SUN	Zalawad Airport
Surat	STV	Surat Airport
Vadodara (Baroda)	BDQ	Vadodara Airport (Civil Airport Harvi)
HIMACHAL PRADESH		
Kangra / Dharamsala	DHM	Gaggal Airport (Kangra Airport)
Kullu / Manali	KUU	Bhuntar Airport (Kullu Manali Airport)
Shimla	SLV	Shimla Airport
JAMMU AND KASHMIR		
Jammu	IXJ	Jammu Airport (Satwari Airport)
Leh	IXL	Leh Kushok Bakula Rimpochee Airport
Srinagar	SXR	Srinagar Airport

City	Code	Airport Name
JHARKHAND		
Jamshedpur	IXW	Jamshedpur Airport
Ranchi	IXR	Birsa Munda Airport (Ranchi Airport)
KARNATAKA		
Bangalore (International)	BLR	Bengaluru International Airport
Belgaum	IXG	Belgaum Airport
Bellary	BEP	Bellary Airport
Mangalore	IXE	Mangalore International Airport
Mysore	MYQ	Mandkalli Airport
KERALA		
Kochi (Cochin) (International)	COK	Cochin International Airport
Kozhikode (Calicut)	CCJ	Calicut International Airport (Karipur Airport)
Thiruvananthapuram (International)	TRV	Trivandrum International Airport
LAKSHADWEEP (UNION TERRITORY)		
Agatti Island	AGX	Agatti Aerodrome
MADHYA PRADESH		
Bhopal	BHO	Bhopal Airport (Bairagarh Airport, Raja Bhoj Airport)
Gwalior	GWL	Gwalior Airport
Indore	IDR	Devi Ahilyabai Holkar Airport
Jabalpur	JLR	Jabalpur Airport
Khajuraho	HJR	Khajuraho Airport
Satna	TNI	Satna Airport
MAHARASHTRA		
Akola	AKD	Akola Airport
Aurangabad	IXU	Aurangabad Airport (Chikkalthana Airport)
Kolhapur	KLH	Kolhapur Airport
Mumbai (Bombay) (International)	BOM	Chhatrapati Shivaji International Airport
Nagpur	NAG	Dr. Babasaheb Ambedkar International Airport
Pune	PNQ	Pune International Airport (Lohegaon Airport)
Ratnagiri	RTC	Ratnagiri Airport
Solapur (Sholapur)	SSE	Sholapur Airport
MANIPUR		
Imphal	IMF	Imphal Airport (Tulihal Airport)

City	*Code*	*Airport Name*
MEGHALAYA		
Rupsi	RUP	Rupsi Airport
Shillong	SHL	Shillong Airport (Barapani Airport, Umroi Airport)
MIZORAM		
Aizawl	AJL	Lengpui Airport
NAGALAND		
Dimapur	DMU	Dimapur Airport
ORISSA		
Bhubaneswar	BBI	Biju Patnaik Airport (Bhubaneswar Airport)
Rourkela	RRK	Rourkela Airport
PUDUCHERRY (UNION TERRITORY)		
Puducherry	PNY	Pondicherry Airport
PUNJAB		
Amritsar (International)	ATQ	Raja Sansi International Airport
Bathinda (Bhatinda)	BUP	Bhisiana Air Force Base
Ludhiana	LUH	Sahnewal Airport
Pathankot	IXP	Pathankot Air Force Base
RAJASTHAN		
Bikaner	BKB	Nal Airport
Jaipur	JAI	Jaipur Airport (Sanganer, Sanganeer Airport)
Jaisalmer	JSA	Jaisalmer Airport
Jodhpur	JDH	Jodhpur Airport
Kota	KTU	Kota Airport
Udaipur	UDR	Udaipur Airport (Maharana Pratap Airport)
TAMIL NADU		
Chennai (International)	MAA	Chennai International Airport (Meenambakkam Airport)
Coimbatore	CJB	Coimbatore Airport (Peelamedu Airport)
Madurai	IXM	Madurai Airport
Salem	SXV	Salem Airport
Tiruchirapalli (Trichy)	TRZ	Tiruchirapalli Airport
Thoothukudi (Tuticorin)	TCR	Tuticorin Airport (Tuticorin Southwest Airport)

City	Code	Airport Name
TRIPURA		
Agartala	IXA	Agartala Airport (Singerbhil Airport)
Kailashahar	IXH	Kailashahar Airport
Kamalpur	IXQ	Kamalpur Airport
Khowai	IXN	Khowai Airport
UTTARAKHAND		
Dehradun	DED	Jolly Grant Airport (Dehradun Airport)
Pant Nagar / Nainital	PGH	Pant Nagar Airport
UTTAR PRADESH		
Agra	AGR	Agra Airport (Kheria Airport)
Allahabad	IXD	Allahabad Airport
Gorakhpur	GOP	Gorakhpur Airport
Kanpur	KNU	Kanpur Airport
Lucknow	LKO	Amausi International Airport
Varanasi	VNS	Varanasi Airport (Babatpur Airport)
WEST BENGAL		
Siliguri	IXB	Bagdogra Airport
Balurghat	RGH	Balurghat Airport
Cooch Behar	COH	Cooch Behar Airport
Kolkata	CCU	Netaji Subhash Chandra Bose International Airport
Malda (English Bazar)	LDA	Malda Airport

LIST OF COUNTRIES WITH NO AIRPORT

Out of the 195 Independent States, only five have no airport included within their boundaries. All of these are in Europe, and all apart from Monaco are landlocked or double landlocked.

Country	Notes
1. **Liechtenstein**	Currently, Liechtenstein only has a heliport in the southern town of Balzers. The nearest international airports are St. Gallen-Altenrhein Airport in Switzerland and Friedrichshafen Airport in Germany, which have few scheduled flights. The nearest major airport is Zurich Airport in Switzerland, which has rail services to Buchs and Sargans. From these towns, it is possible to catch a Postal Bus to Liechtenstein.
2. **Andorra**	There is no airport in Andorra. The nearest airports are in Lleida, Barcelona, Toulouse and Girona. By both population and by land area, Andorra is the largest country not to have an airport. However, there is one heliport.
3. **Vatican City**	The nearest airport to the Vatican City is Leonardo da Vinci-Fiumicino Airport. It would be physically impossible to fit a whole airport into the 0.44km^2 land area of the Holy See, but there is a heliport located in the western corner, which is used for visiting heads and officials of the city-state.
4. **San Marino**	San Marino does not currently have an airport; instead, there is a heliport located at Borgo Maggiore. The nearest airport is in Rimini, Italy.
5. **Monaco**	Monaco does not have an airport, but there is a heliport located in the Monagasque district of Fontvieille. The nearest airport to Monaco is Cote d'Azur Airport in Nice, France.

★★★

27. Instrument Landing System (ILS)

AN instrument landing system (ILS) is a ground-based instrument approach system that provides precision guidance to an aircraft approaching and landing on a runway, using a combination of radio signals and, in many cases, high-intensity lighting arrays to enable a safe landing during Instrument Meteorological Conditions (IMC), such as low ceilings or reduced visibility due to fog, rain, or blowing snow.

Instrument Approach Procedure charts (or approach plates) are published for each ILS approach, providing pilots with the needed information to fly an ILS approach during Instrument Flight Rules (IFR) operations, including the radio frequencies used by the ILS components or navaids and the minimum visibility requirements prescribed for the specific approach.

Radio-navigation aids must keep a certain degree of accuracy (set by international standards of Commercial Aviation Safety Team (CAST)/International Civil Aviation Organisation (ICAO); to assure this is the case, flight inspection organizations periodically check critical parameters with properly equipped aircraft to calibrate and certify ILS precision.

USE OF ILS

At controlled airports, air traffic control will direct aircraft to the localizer via assigned headings, making sure aircraft do not get too close to each other (maintain separation), but also avoiding delay as much as possible. Several aircraft can be on the ILS at the same time, several miles apart. An aircraft that has come within two and a half degrees of the localizer course (half scale deflection shown by the course deviation indicator) is said to be established on the approach. Typically, an aircraft will be established by at least two miles prior to the final approach fix (glideslope intercept at the specified altitude).

Aircraft deviation from the optimal path is indicated to the flight crew by means of display dial (a carry over from when an analog meter movement would indicate deviation from the course line via voltages sent from the ILS receiver).

The output from the ILS receiver goes both to the display system (head-down display and head-up display, if installed) and can also go to the Flight Control Computer. An aircraft landing procedure can be either coupled, where the Flight Control Computer directly flies the aircraft and the flight crew monitor the operation; or uncoupled (manual) where the flight crew fly the aircraft uses the HUD and manually control the aircraft to minimize the deviation from flight path to the runway centreline.

ILS CATEGORIES

There are three categories of ILS which support similarly named categories of operation. The category of ILS describe the tolerance and precision. Information below is based on ICAO - certain states may have filed differences.

- **Category I (CAT I):** A precision instrument approach and landing with a decision height not lower than 200 feet (61 m) above touchdown zone elevation and with either a visibility not less than 800 meters (2,625 ft) or a runway visual range (RVR) not less than 550 meters (1,804 ft). Not much use in dense fog.
- **Category II (CAT II):** A precision instrument approach and landing with a decision height lower than 200 feet (61 m) above touchdown zone elevation but not lower than 100 feet (30 m), and a runway visual range not less than 300 meters (984 ft) for aircraft category A, B, C and not less than 350 meters (1,148 ft) for aircraft category D.
- **Category III (CAT III)** is further subdivided
  - Category III A - A precision instrument approach and landing with:
    - *(a)* a decision height lower than 100 feet (30 m) above touchdown zone elevation, or no decision height; and
    - *(b)* a runway visual range not less than 200 meters (656 ft).
  - Category III B - A precision instrument approach and landing with:
    - *(a)* a decision height lower than 50 feet (15 m) above touchdown zone elevation, or no decision height; and
    - *(b)* a runway visual range less than 200 meters (656 ft) but not less than 75 meters (246 ft). Autopilot is used until taxi-speed.
  - Category III C - A precision instrument approach and landing with no decision height and no runway visual range limitations. You can land blind, even cover up the cockpit windows with black paper, sit back, and land. In practice, no airport allows CAT IIIC landing yet, because of practical issues–like how do you taxi off the runway if you can't see a thing?

Pilots can't do much manually in dense fog. So aircraft use automatic landing or Autoland. Even after touchdown, the system runs the aircraft: spoilers, autobrakes with ABS, and thrust reversers kick in... When it slows down, control is handed over to the pilot, who then has to taxi the aircraft very carefully, and avoid bumping into other aircraft....

In each case a suitably equipped aircraft and appropriately qualified crew are required. For example, Cat IIIb requires a fail-operational system, along with a crew who are qualified and current, Cat I does not. A head-up display which allows the pilot to perform aircraft maneuvers rather than an automatic system is considered as fail-operational. Cat I relies only on altimeter indications for decision height, whereas Cat II and Cat III approaches use radar altimeter to determine decision height.

An ILS is required to shut down upon internal detection of a fault condition as mentioned in the monitoring section. With the increasing categories, ILS equipment is required to shut down faster since higher categories require shorter response times. For example, a Cat I localizer must shutdown within 10 seconds of detecting a fault, but a Cat III localizer must shut down in less than 2 seconds.

28. Airports Authority of India (AAI)

Airports Authority of India (AAI) manages 124 airports, which include 12 international airports, 81 domestic airports and 23 civil enclaves at Defence airfields and 8 Custom airports. AAI also provides Air Traffic Management Services over entire Indian Air Space and adjoining oceanic areas with ground installations at all airports and 25 other locations to ensure safety of aircraft operations.

AAI is the pride of the country, for it is one of the main catalysts contributing towards its economic growth. To substantiate the statement it would but be prudent to lay due emphasis on the fact, that the list of the key industries responsible include Airports and Aviation sector.

At present AAI is focussing on developing second line airports across the country & in remote corners. Accordingly, plans have been drawn for new terminals at 35 airports, and runway/apron expansion at 23 airports. In 2002-03 AAI around 55 active airports as compared to more than 90 as on date. In terms of investment, in the Tenth Plan it was around Rs. 40 billion and in the Eleventh Plan it is Rs. 400 billion, a four fold increase.

35 Metro Airports Under Development

- Ahmedabad, Amritsar, Agatti, Aurangabad, Agartala, *Agra*,
- Baroda, Bhopal, Bhubaneshwar, Chandigarh, Coimbatore,
- Dehradun, Dimapur, Goa (Dabolim), Guwahati,
- Imphal, Indore, Jaipur, Jammu, Khajuraho, Madurai, Mangalore
- Lucknow, Nagpur, Patna, Portblair, Pune, Rajkot, Ranchi, Raipur,
- Trichy, Trivandrum, Udaipur, Visakhapatnam, Varanasi

Completed–09
Work in Progress–26

The profit for AAI during year 2008 - 09 (RE) has been Rs. 687.21. However, the Revenue Turnover of AAI as on 1st November, 2009 was Rs. 2286.53 crores.

OTHER 23 AIRPORTS UNDER DEVELOPMENT

- Dibrugarh
- Srinagar
- Calicut
- Kullu
- Surat
- Rajahmundry
- Vijayawada
- Hubli
- Belgaum
- Cooch Behar
- Mysore
- Akola
- Gondia
- Jodhpur
- Cuddapah
- Shillong
- Tezu
- Jaisalmer
- Poundicherry
- Leh
- Pant Nagar
- Jorhat
- Bhavnagar

Competed–12
Work in progress-11

In addition to the above 58 airports identified for development, AAI has two major projects at Kolkata and Chennai airports.

29. Some More Facts & Figures

WORLD AIRLINE TRAFFIC

January-November 2009

US	2009	2008	% chg
RPKs (mil.)	1,044,080	1,113,428	-6.2
ASKs (mil.)	1,296,371	1,391,785	-6.9
Pass. (000)	592,100	631,900	-6.3
Pass. LF (%)	80.5	80.0	0.5
FTKs (mil.)	63,541	92,146	-31.0

Europe	2009	2008	% chg
RPKs (mil.)	689,784	725,325	-4.9
ASKs (mil.)	907,122	947,881	-4.3
Pass. (000)	301,839	322,130	-6.3
Pass. LF (%)	76.0	76.5	-0.5
FTKs (mil.)	27,998	34,144	-18.0

Asia Pacific	2009	2008	% chg
RPKs (mil.)	502,670	544,537	-7.7
ASKs (mil.)	677,265	724,028	-6.5
Pass. (000)	120,729	129,727	-6.9
Pass. LF (%)	74.2	75.2	-1.0
FTKs (mil.)	42,353	49,059	-13.7

Latin America	2009	2008	% chg
RPKs (mil.)	161,735	158,386	2.1
ASKs (mil.)	230,445	222,206	3.7
Pass. (000)	111,726	108,877	2.6
Pass. LF (%)	70.2	71.3	-1.1
FTKs (mil.)	2,775	2,983	-7.0

RPKs — Revenue-Passenger-Kilometers
ASKs — Available Seat Kilometres
Pass. LF — Passenger Load Factor
FTKs — Freight Ton Kilometers

IATA FUEL PRICE ANALYSIS — JANUARY 1, 2010

	Share in World Index	cts./gal.	$/bbl	$/mt	Index Value 2000 = 100
Jet Fuel Price	**100%**	**210.5**	**88.4**	**696.7**	**241.7**
Asia & Oceania	22%	209.5	88.0	695.0	251.4
Europe & CIS	28%	208.9	87.7	691.3	236.3
Middle East & Africa	7%	202.1	84.9	669.6	253.4
North America	39%	212.8	89.4	705.3	237.6
Latin & Central America	4%	219.3	92.1	709.1	255.1

TOP 20 AIRLINES SYSTEM TRAFFIC

January-December 2009

Rank	Airline	RPKS	Rank	Airline	RPKS
1	Delta *	304,025,157	11	Qantas Group[1]	91,056,000
2	Air France KLM	202,010,000	12	Cathay Pacific	89,440,308
3	American	196,904,216	13	Singapore Airlines	81,552,000
4	United	161,663,594	14	Air Canada	77,045,000
5	Continental	128,436,623	15	Japan Airlines[1]	67,959,571
6	Lufthansa	122,991,000	16	Iberia	49,612,000
7	Southwest	119,800,861	17	Thai Airways[1]	47,477,000
8	Emirates[1]	107,058,026	18	Korean Air[2]	42,957,486
9	British Airways	104,865,000	19	JetBlue	41,762,234
10	US Airways	93,146,251	20	Virgin Atlantic[2]	34,279,200

*1. January-Nov. 2. January-Oct. *Includes Northwest Airlines; Regional operations.*

World Airport Traffic—November 2009

	INTERNATIONAL		DOMESTIC		TOTAL	
	Pass . (000)	% chg.	Pass . (000)	% chg.	Pass . (000)	% chg.
Africa	5,397	4.4	2,807	0.4	8,265	2.8
Asia/Pacific	28,325	10.0	41,856	9.5	71,044	9.5
Europe	55,333	-0.4	19,598	3.6	75,228	0.6
Latin Am./Carib.	3,947	2.3	10,293	21.0	14,747	14.9
Middle East	7,656	13.1		8,008	11.5	
North America	12,222	-1.4	69,750	1.6	82,041	1.0
Total	**112,881**	**3.1**	**144,304**	**5.3**	**259,332**	**4.2**

Passenger Traffic 2008*

Rank	*City (Airport)*	*Total Passengers*	*% Change*
1	ATLANTA GA (ATL)	90 039 280	0.7
2	CHICAGO IL (ORD)	69 353 876	(9.0)
3	LONDON (LHR)	67 056 379	(1.5)
4	TOKYO (HND)	66 754 829	(0.2)
5	PARIS (CDG)	60 874 681	1.6
6	LOS ANGELES CA (LAX)	59 497 539	(4.7)
7	DALLAS/FORT WORTH TX (DFW)	57 093 187	(4.5)
8	BEIJING (PEK)	55 937 289	4.4
9	FRANKFURT (FRA)	53 467 450	(1.3)
10	DENVER CO (DEN)	51 245 334	

**Updated in July 2009*

LARGEST AIRLINES OF THE WORLD

American Airlines

Country: USA

Largest airline of the world ranked by traffic, domestic services in the USA and wide international operations.

Air France - KLM

Country: France - Netherlands

Newly established airline group is ranked as the largest in Europe, global scheduled services via Amsterdam and Paris hubs.

United Airlines

Country: USA

Third largest airline in the world by traffic, regular domestic and international services.

Delta Air Lines

Country: USA

World's largest airline by carried passenger number, scheduled services from its huge Atlanta hub.

Southwest Airlines

Country: USA

World's largest budget airline, widest route network in the United States.

SkyWest Airlines

Country: USA

World's largest regional airline, extended feeder services to the U.S. major airlines networks.

Thomson Airways

Country: United Kingdom

World's largest charter airline, passenger international services to holiday destinations from UK and continental Europe.

British Airways

Country: United Kingdom

Largest airline of the Great Britain, short and long-range operations from its London bases.

Lufthansa

Country: Germany

Largest airline of Germany, global scheduled services via Frankfurt and Munich hubs.

Japan Airlines

Country: Japan

Largest airline of Asia, mostly long-range operations from Tokyo.

GLOBAL AIRLINE ALLIANCES

Star Alliance

Largest global alliance headed by American United Airlines, German Lufthansa and Japanese All Nippon Airways.

SkyTeam

Global alliance driven by American Delta Air Lines, Continental and Northwest and the European largest AirFrance-KLM.

Oneworld

Alliance combines networks of the world's largest American Airlines, British Airways in Europe, Asian Japan Airlines and Qantas in Australia.

Passenger Airlines (By Fleet Size)

Rank	Airline	Fleet Size
1.	Delta Air Lines	752
2.	American Airlines	612
3.	Air France-KLM	607
4.	Southwest Airlines	547
5.	United Airlines	359
6.	US Airways	357
7.	Continental Airlines	338
8.	Lufthansa	331
9.	China Southern Airlines	324
10.	SkyWest Airlines	286
11.	British Airways	248

Cargo Airlines

Rank	Airline	Fleet Size
1.	FedEx Express	672
2.	DHL Aviation	350
3.	UPS Airlines	262

30. Indian Aviation Sector : Present Scenario

Aviation sectors all over the world had suffered setbacks in 2008-2009 due to global recession, fuel prices and load factor, with hopes of seeing a revival in 2011. But the presence of a strong domestic market helped most Indian industry sectors including aviation, survive the recession. Figures from recent months suggest the Indian economy is heading in the right direction, as the domestic airline industry, which was sluggish only a few months back, appears to be in its recovery mode.

ONE of the fastest growing aviation industries in the world, the Indian aviation sector, which comprises private airline companies accounting for more than 75 per cent, has been witnessing a compound annual growth rate of 18 per cent. The industry currently has 454 airports, including 16 international ones, and was hoping to see revival by 2011 after the recession and slump in tourism. But now, revival doesn't seem as distant after the final quarter of 2009 raised industry hopes by recording growth in passenger numbers. There was a drop of 30 per cent in passenger load factor leading to losses in many top airlines in the world including British Airways; the last quarter of 2009 has again raised some hopes of revival in the country. The increase in air traffic movement towards the end of 2009, especially in the month of December, increased industry revenues by over USD 20 million. Signs of recovery for the aviation sector in India can be gauged from the increase in domestic travel in the last quarter.

> In a positive sign for the aviation industry, which has been going a through a bad patch, air traffic for the first two months of the year showed a growth of 19.2 per cent as compared with the same period last year. Passengers carried by domestic airlines from Jan-Feb were 80.6 lakh as against 67.6 lakh in the corresponding period of 2009.

Airlines in India carried a record 44.9 lakh passengers in December 2009, a number that also helped airline companies maintain better yields and prevented them from selling seats below cost. Flying high on strong economic recovery, domestic air travel has made a comeback in 2009, with traffic registering an increase of 7.9% over the previous year. In 2008, air traffic fell by 5% with

412 lakh domestic fliers taking to skies against 433 lakh in 2007. The increase to 445.1 lakh flyers in 2009 came on the strong revival in traffic since July, as the first six months were consistently witnessing a double digit percentage fall.

December 2009 saw a whopping 33% increase with 44.9 lakh people flying within India as compared to 33.7 lakh in December 2008.

Developments

The Hyderabad International Airport, managed by a public-private joint venture consisting of the GMR Group, Malaysia Airports Holdings Berhad and both the State Government of Andhra Pradesh and Airports Authority of India (AAI), has been ranked amongst the world's top five in the annual Airport Service Quality (ASQ) passenger survey along with airports at Seoul, Singapore, Hong Kong and Beijing. In addition to creating global standards international airports in Delhi and Mumbai, the Airports Authority of India (AAI) is also developing the airports in Kolkata and Chennai with an investment of USD 427.5 million and USD 384.7 million respectively. The AAI is also looking at upgrading and modernising 35 non-metro airports; while the government is looking at building infrastructure in terms of air traffic control (ATC) and CNS systems. Safety and surveillance is another huge area being worked upon.

Future Progress

According to the report by Investment Commission of India (ICI), the future for Indian aviation up to the year 2020 has been estimated to create investment opportunities in excess of USD 100 billion, with USD 80 billion in new aircrafts and around USD 30 billion in the development of airport infrastructure.

The state of Punjab will become the first state in the country to set up a Maintenance, Repair and Overhaul (MRO) hub at Ropar, for the civil aviation sector at a cost of USD 6.4 million. Similarly, prominent aircraft manufacturer Boeing is planning on setting up a MRO facility in New Delhi at a proposed investment of USD 100 million. North India will also receive it's first private sector 'greenfield' international airport; named Aerotropolis. Celebi Holding, one of the largest business conglomerates from Turkey, has further cemented its foothold in Indian aviation industry after bagging contracts for Delhi International Airport Private Ltd. and Mumbai International Airport. The company aims to invest USD 100 million by 2010 end. The country's first SEZ dedicated to the Aerospace sector at Hattaragi, 37 km from Belgaum, in Karnataka has also been inaugurated. The SEZ is spread over 300 acres of land and is being brought up with an investment of USD 32 million in. An Aerospace and Precision Engineering Special Economic Zone with a proposed investment of USD 641 million has also come up at Adibatla, Ranga Reddy district, Andhra Pradesh.

A Mixed Feeling

No-frills airlines IndiGo and SpiceJet are aggressively adding to their fleet in February, 2010 while their full-service counterparts Air India, Kingfisher and Jet Airways are cutting capacity after tough couple of years, indicating a difference of opinion in the industry over future prospects.

The domestic airlines are estimated to have lost over $3 billion (Rs 14,000 crore) in the past two years mainly on account of sharp drop in demand growth, excess capacity, high fuel prices and at times irrational pricing by airlines to fill the excess capacity.

Delhi-based IndiGo has recently sought the government permission to import 10 Airbus 320 jets to be deployed on various domestic routes in the coming months. The airline recently launched Re 1 fare (exclusive of fuel surcharge and taxes) on several routes.

The Indian airline industry contributes over 20% to the global airline industry's losses while having only 2% share in the world air traffic.

In the past nine months, all the three full-service carriers have put in additional seats by converting their two-class configured jet into single class. This way they have managed to keep their operational cost and fleet size same while adding capacity in the market.

SpiceJet has submitted its application to import three B737s to the empowered committee on aircraft acquisition in the civil aviation ministry. The airline wants to add three more jets to its fleet by the end of next month.

The domestic air traffic has grown over 20% in the past few months, but on a low base of the past year. Demand is expected to soften in the coming lean season. The airlines are currently managing to fill only 75-80% of their seats, which means there is still additional capacity in the market.

Faced with cash crunch, SpiceJet had earlier roped in WL Ross & Co to invest in the company. After the financial crisis caused aviation growth to falter, state-owned Air India had decided to trim its fleet size to the extent of 30% to 105 jets by 2011. Kingfisher has already cut capacity reducing its fleet to 68 aircraft from 89 earlier. Besides deferring deliveries of aircraft, Jet Airways is negotiating with royal Brunei Airlines to lease out three B777s.